Macmillan First Atlas

Written and designed by

Nicola Wright · Tony Potter · Dee Turner · Christine Wilson

Illustrated by

Lyn Mitchell

Contents

Macmillan Publishing Company
New York

Maxwell Macmillan International
New York Oxford Singapore Sydney

Maxwell Macmillan Canada
Toronto

All about maps

A map is a picture of a place from above. Imagine what your home would look like if you flew over it in an airplane and took a photograph. The picture would show the area around your home spread out flat.

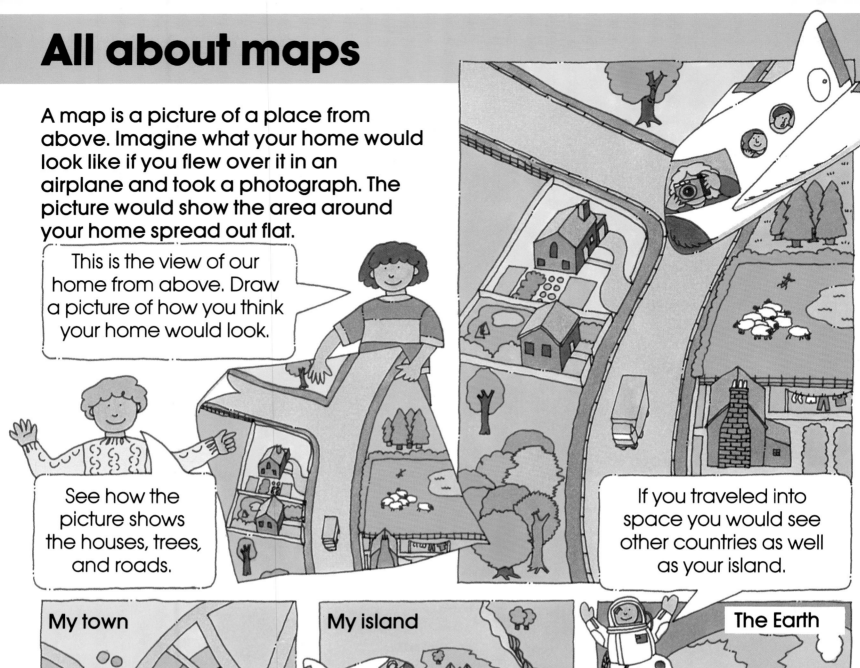

This is the view of our home from above. Draw a picture of how you think your home would look.

See how the picture shows the houses, trees, and roads.

If you traveled into space you would see other countries as well as your island.

My town

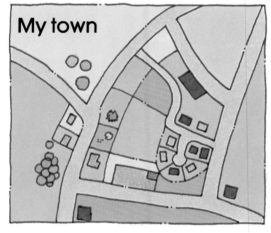

Imagine that you fly higher. Now you can see your whole town or city. Everything looks tiny.

My island

Imagine your town is on an island. As you go even higher you can see the whole island.

The Earth

Clouds form in the sky and swirl around the Earth. There is much more ocean than land.

This is how my island would look as a map. Tiny pictures called symbols are used to stand for real things.

The pictures below are the symbols used in this book. This part of an atlas is called the **legend**. The legend tells you what the symbols stand for.

Looking for a country? Here is what to do: Go to the list on page 40 and look under the first letter of the country name. So, **Chile** is under the letter **C**.

 **Country boundaries**

 **Oceans and Seas**

 **Capital cities** ■ Moscow

Large cities ● Vladivostok

 **Lakes**

Rivers

 **High mountains**

Low mountains

 **Tropical rain forest**

 **Monsoon woodland** (hot areas with a rainy season)

 **Pine forest**

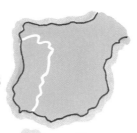 **Leafy woodland**

 **Mixed woodland**

Mediterranean woodland (dry areas with evergreen trees)

Desert (some deserts are just sandy, but some are stony and covered with bushes or cacti)

Grassland (called **prairie** in North America, and **pampas** in South America)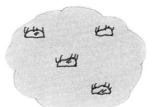

Steppe (scrubland or grassland in Asia)

Savannah (dry grasslands with some trees in Africa)

Tundra (frozen land)

Ice

3

World map

This big map shows the world as though its round shape has been flattened out. The differently colored areas of land are called continents. There are seven continents and four oceans.

This is planet Earth. Imagine a line around its middle. This is called the equator.

This book shows you some of the people, animals, plants, and places found in each continent.

The biggest continent is Asia. The smallest continent is Australia.

Countries

The maps in this book show all the countries in the world. A white line shows where one country joins another.

Every country has a flag. Some of them are shown in this book.

Arctic Ocean

North America

Atlantic Ocean

Equator

Pacific Ocean

South America

Atlantic Ocean

The bottom half of the world is called the southern hemisphere.

South Pole

The Polish flag
The Belgian flag
The Czechoslovakian flag
The Irish flag.

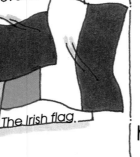

4

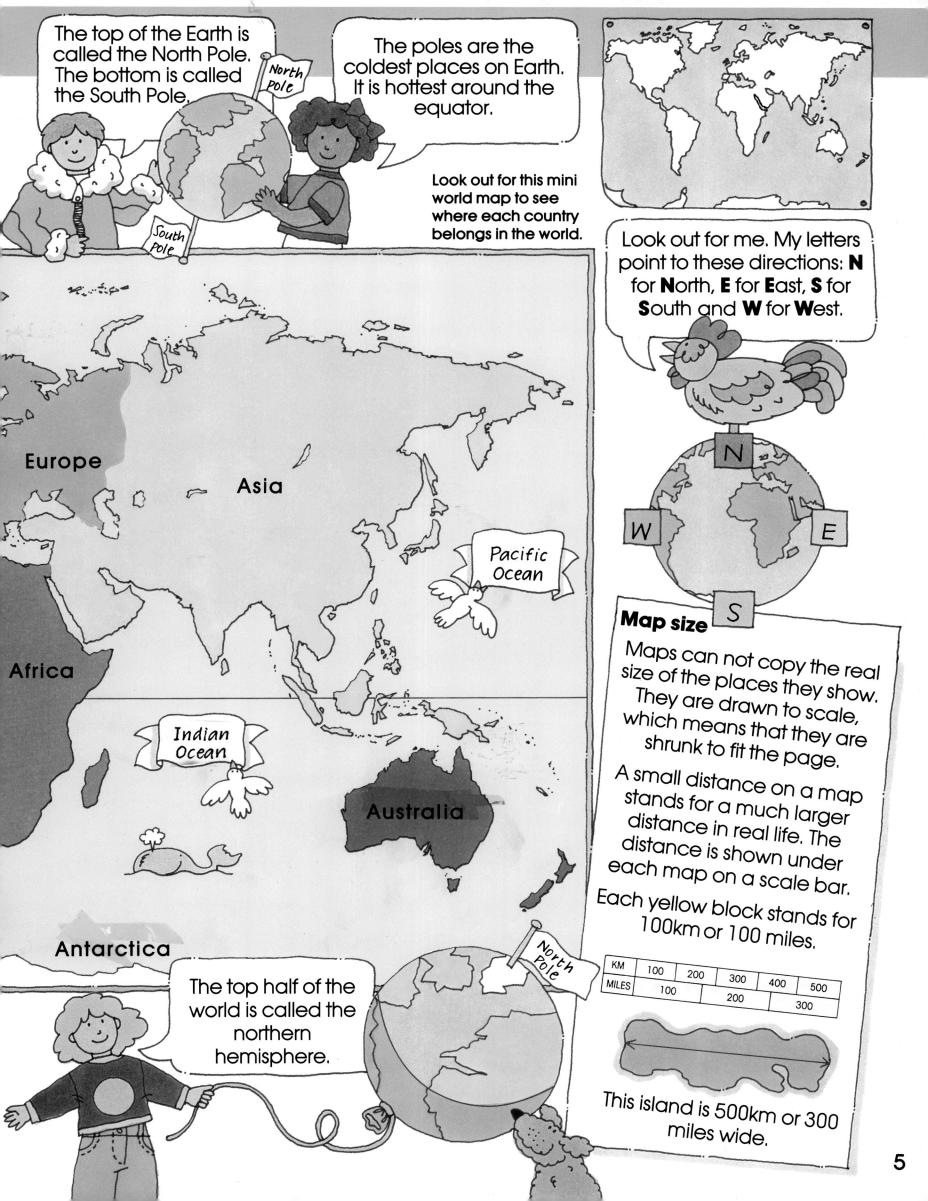

The top of the Earth is called the North Pole. The bottom is called the South Pole.

North pole

South pole

The poles are the coldest places on Earth. It is hottest around the equator.

Look out for this mini world map to see where each country belongs in the world.

Look out for me. My letters point to these directions: **N** for **N**orth, **E** for **E**ast, **S** for **S**outh and **W** for **W**est.

N

W   E

S

Europe

Asia

Pacific Ocean

Africa

Indian Ocean

Australia

Antarctica

Map size

Maps can not copy the real size of the places they show. They are drawn to scale, which means that they are shrunk to fit the page.

A small distance on a map stands for a much larger distance in real life. The distance is shown under each map on a scale bar.

Each yellow block stands for 100km or 100 miles.

KM	100	200	300	400	500
MILES	100		200		300

This island is 500km or 300 miles wide.

The top half of the world is called the northern hemisphere.

North Pole

The United States of America

The United States of America is divided into 50 separate states and the District of Columbia. Here you can see each state's boundary and capital city.

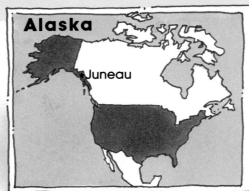

Alaska

Juneau

Alaska is separated from the rest of the U.S. by Canada. It is the largest state, but much of the land is too cold to live on or grow crops. Fishing and oil are the main industries.

More people live in California than in any other state.

Hawaii

★Honolulu

Hawaii is a group of volcanic islands in the middle of the Pacific Ocean. In 1959 it became the 50th state. Its beaches are very popular with tourists.

Pacific Ocean

The spectacular Grand Canyon is in Arizona.

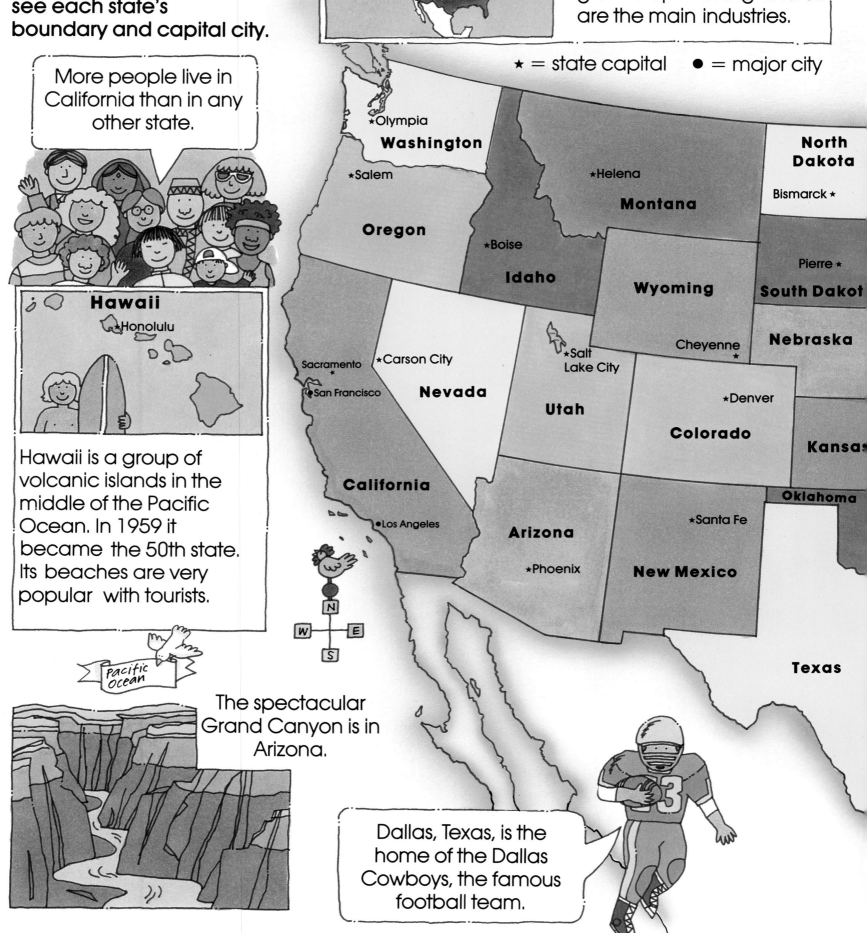

★ = state capital   ● = major city

★Olympia
Washington

★Salem

Oregon

★Helena

Montana

★Boise

Idaho

North Dakota

Bismarck ★

Pierre ★

Wyoming

South Dakot

Cheyenne ★

Nebraska

★Carson City

Sacramento ★

●San Francisco

Nevada

★Salt Lake City

Utah

★Denver

Colorado

Kansa

California

●Los Angeles

N
W   E
S

★Santa Fe

Arizona

★Phoenix

New Mexico

Oklahoma

Texas

Dallas, Texas, is the home of the Dallas Cowboys, the famous football team.

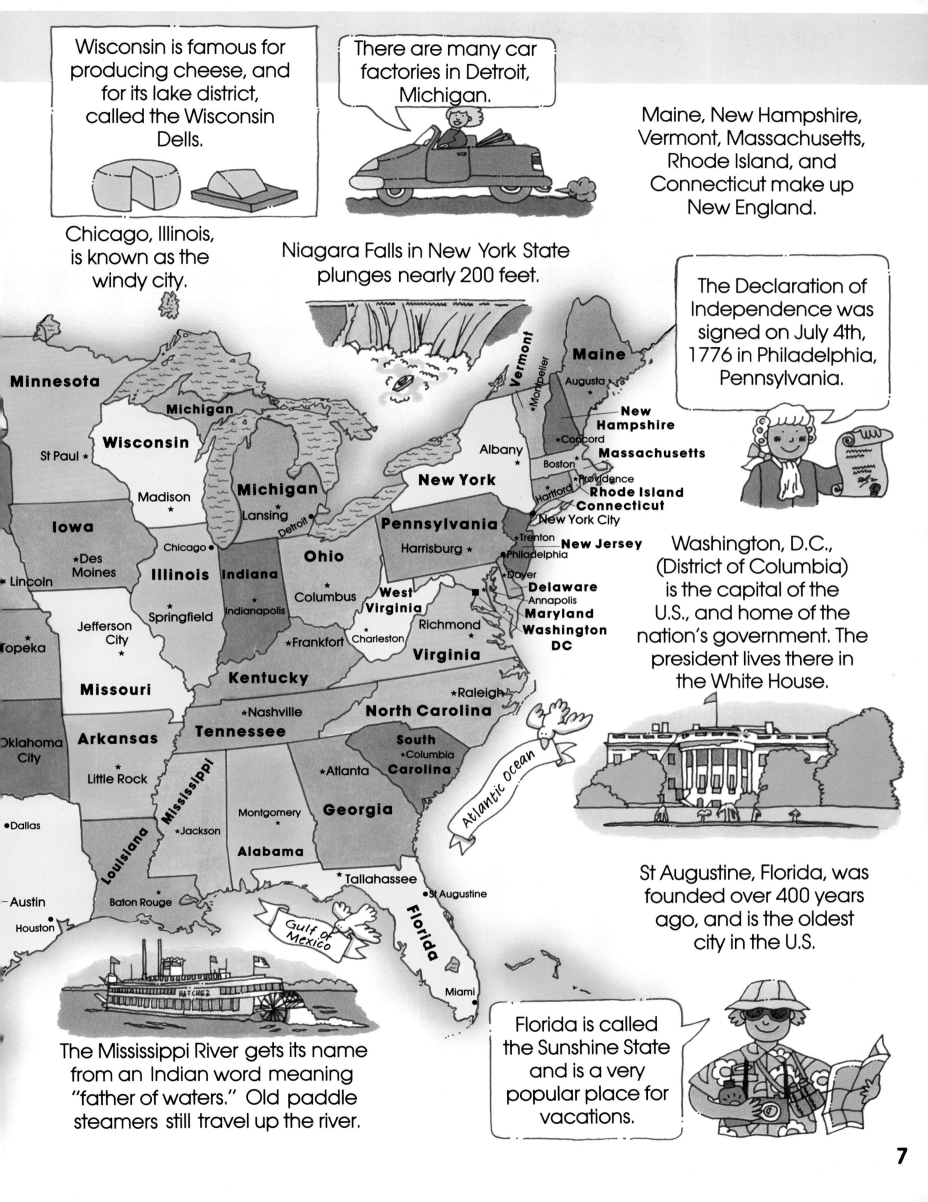

Wisconsin is famous for producing cheese, and for its lake district, called the Wisconsin Dells.

There are many car factories in Detroit, Michigan.

Maine, New Hampshire, Vermont, Massachusetts, Rhode Island, and Connecticut make up New England.

Chicago, Illinois, is known as the windy city.

Niagara Falls in New York State plunges nearly 200 feet.

The Declaration of Independence was signed on July 4th, 1776 in Philadelphia, Pennsylvania.

Washington, D.C., (District of Columbia) is the capital of the U.S., and home of the nation's government. The president lives there in the White House.

St Augustine, Florida, was founded over 400 years ago, and is the oldest city in the U.S.

Florida is called the Sunshine State and is a very popular place for vacations.

The Mississippi River gets its name from an Indian word meaning "father of waters." Old paddle steamers still travel up the river.

Minnesota
Michigan
Wisconsin
St Paul ★
Madison
Michigan
Lansing ★
Detroit ●
Iowa
★ Des Moines
Chicago ●
Illinois
Indiana
★ Springfield
Indianapolis ★
★ Lincoln
Jefferson City ★
Topeka ★
Missouri
Ohio
★ Columbus
West Virginia
★ Frankfort
Charleston ★
Kentucky
★ Nashville
Oklahoma City
Arkansas
Tennessee
★ Little Rock
Mississippi
Louisiana
★ Jackson
Montgomery ★
Alabama
● Dallas
Austin
Baton Rouge ★
Houston ●
Vermont
★ Montpelier
Maine
Augusta ★
New Hampshire
★ Concord
Albany ★
Massachusetts
Boston ★
Providence
Hartford
Rhode Island
Connecticut
New York
New York City
★ Trenton
New Jersey
Pennsylvania
Harrisburg ★
Philadelphia ●
★ Dover
Delaware
Annapolis ●
Maryland
Washington DC
Richmond ★
Virginia
★ Raleigh
North Carolina
South Carolina
★ Columbia
★ Atlanta
Georgia
Atlantic Ocean
Gulf of Mexico
★ Tallahassee
● St Augustine
Florida
Miami ●

7

State flags

Each state has its own capital city, flag, bird, flower, tree, and even song. Here you can see all fifty different state flags. This is what the little pictures beside the flags mean:

☆ state capital

🐦 state bird

🌼 state flower

🌳 state tree

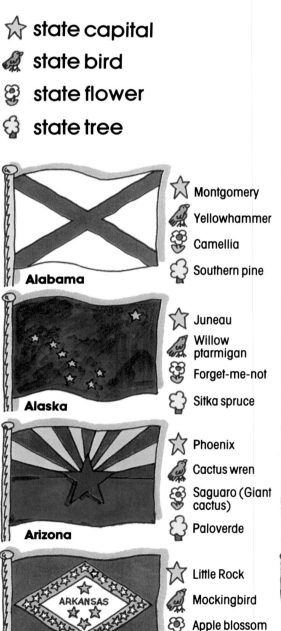

Alabama
- ☆ Montgomery
- 🐦 Yellowhammer
- 🌼 Camellia
- 🌳 Southern pine

Alaska
- ☆ Juneau
- 🐦 Willow ptarmigan
- 🌼 Forget-me-not
- 🌳 Sitka spruce

Arizona
- ☆ Phoenix
- 🐦 Cactus wren
- 🌼 Saguaro (Giant cactus)
- 🌳 Paloverde

Arkansas

- ☆ Little Rock
- 🐦 Mockingbird
- 🌼 Apple blossom
- 🌳 Pine

California
- ☆ Sacramento
- 🐦 California valley quail
- 🌼 Golden poppy
- 🌳 California redwood

Colorado
- ☆ Denver
- 🐦 Lark bunting
- 🌼 Rocky Mountain columbine
- 🌳 Blue spruce

Connecticut

- ☆ Hartford
- 🐦 Robin
- 🌼 Mountain laurel
- 🌳 White Oak

Delaware

- ☆ Dover
- 🐦 Blue hen chicken
- 🌼 Peach blossom
- 🌳 American holly

Florida
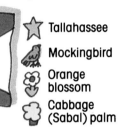
- ☆ Tallahassee
- 🐦 Mockingbird
- 🌼 Orange blossom
- 🌳 Cabbage (Sabal) palm

Georgia

- ☆ Atlanta
- 🐦 Brown thrasher
- 🌼 Cherokee rose
- 🌳 Live oak

Hawaii
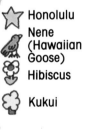
- ☆ Honolulu
- 🐦 Nene (Hawaiian Goose)
- 🌼 Hibiscus
- 🌳 Kukui

Idaho

- ☆ Boise
- 🐦 Mountain bluebird
- 🌼 Syringa (Mock orange)
- 🌳 Western white pine

Illinois
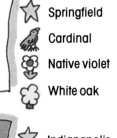
- ☆ Springfield
- 🐦 Cardinal
- 🌼 Native violet
- 🌳 White oak

Indiana

- ☆ Indianapolis
- 🐦 Cardinal
- 🌼 Peony
- 🌳 Tulip tree (Yellow poplar)

Iowa
- ☆ Des Moines
- 🐦 Eastern goldfinch
- 🌼 Wild rose
- 🌳 Oak

Kansas

- ☆ Topeka
- 🐦 Western meadow lark
- 🌼 Sunflower
- 🌳 Cottonwood

Kentucky

- ☆ Frankfort
- 🐦 Kentucky cardinal
- 🌼 Goldenrod
- 🌳 Kentucky coffeetree

Louisiana

- ☆ Baton Rouge
- 🐦 Brown pelican
- 🌼 Magnolia
- 🌳 Bald cypress

Maine
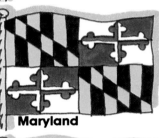
- ☆ Augusta
- 🐦 Chickadee
- 🌼 White pine cone & tassel
- 🌳 White pine

Maryland

- ☆ Annapolis
- 🐦 Baltimore oriole
- 🌼 Black-eyed Susan
- 🌳 White oak (Wye oak)

Massachusetts
 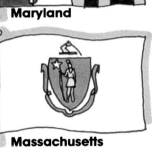
- ☆ Boston
- 🐦 Chickadee
- 🌼 Arbutus (Mayflower)
- 🌳 American elm

Michigan

- ☆ Lansing
- 🐦 Robin
- 🌼 Apple blossom
- 🌳 White pine

Minnesota

- ☆ St. Paul
- 🐦 Common loon
- 🌼 Pink & white lady's-slipper
- 🌳 Norway, or red, pine

8

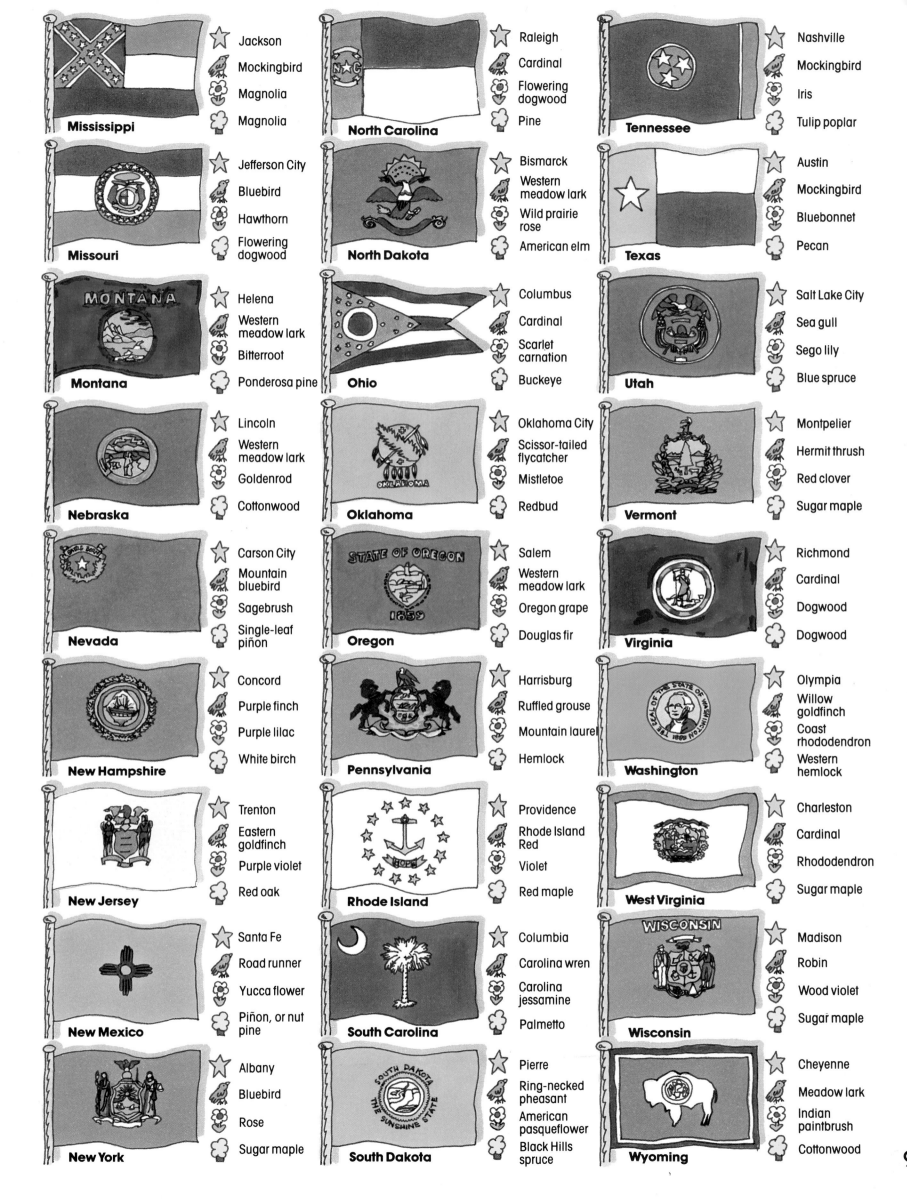

Mississippi
- ⭐ Jackson
- 🐦 Mockingbird
- 🌼 Magnolia
- 🌳 Magnolia

Missouri
- ⭐ Jefferson City
- 🐦 Bluebird
- 🌼 Hawthorn
- 🌳 Flowering dogwood

Montana
- ⭐ Helena
- 🐦 Western meadow lark
- 🌼 Bitterroot
- 🌳 Ponderosa pine

Nebraska
- ⭐ Lincoln
- 🐦 Western meadow lark
- 🌼 Goldenrod
- 🌳 Cottonwood

Nevada
- ⭐ Carson City
- 🐦 Mountain bluebird
- 🌼 Sagebrush
- 🌳 Single-leaf piñon

New Hampshire
- ⭐ Concord
- 🐦 Purple finch
- 🌼 Purple lilac
- 🌳 White birch

New Jersey
- ⭐ Trenton
- 🐦 Eastern goldfinch
- 🌼 Purple violet
- 🌳 Red oak

New Mexico
- ⭐ Santa Fe
- 🐦 Road runner
- 🌼 Yucca flower
- 🌳 Piñon, or nut pine

New York
- ⭐ Albany
- 🐦 Bluebird
- 🌼 Rose
- 🌳 Sugar maple

North Carolina
- ⭐ Raleigh
- 🐦 Cardinal
- 🌼 Flowering dogwood
- 🌳 Pine

North Dakota
- ⭐ Bismarck
- 🐦 Western meadow lark
- 🌼 Wild prairie rose
- 🌳 American elm

Ohio
- ⭐ Columbus
- 🐦 Cardinal
- 🌼 Scarlet carnation
- 🌳 Buckeye

Oklahoma
- ⭐ Oklahoma City
- 🐦 Scissor-tailed flycatcher
- 🌼 Mistletoe
- 🌳 Redbud

Oregon
- ⭐ Salem
- 🐦 Western meadow lark
- 🌼 Oregon grape
- 🌳 Douglas fir

Pennsylvania
- ⭐ Harrisburg
- 🐦 Ruffled grouse
- 🌼 Mountain laurel
- 🌳 Hemlock

Rhode Island
- ⭐ Providence
- 🐦 Rhode Island Red
- 🌼 Violet
- 🌳 Red maple

South Carolina
- ⭐ Columbia
- 🐦 Carolina wren
- 🌼 Carolina jessamine
- 🌳 Palmetto

South Dakota
- ⭐ Pierre
- 🐦 Ring-necked pheasant
- 🌼 American pasqueflower
- 🌳 Black Hills spruce

Tennessee
- ⭐ Nashville
- 🐦 Mockingbird
- 🌼 Iris
- 🌳 Tulip poplar

Texas
- ⭐ Austin
- 🐦 Mockingbird
- 🌼 Bluebonnet
- 🌳 Pecan

Utah
- ⭐ Salt Lake City
- 🐦 Sea gull
- 🌼 Sego lily
- 🌳 Blue spruce

Vermont
- ⭐ Montpelier
- 🐦 Hermit thrush
- 🌼 Red clover
- 🌳 Sugar maple

Virginia
- ⭐ Richmond
- 🐦 Cardinal
- 🌼 Dogwood
- 🌳 Dogwood

Washington
- ⭐ Olympia
- 🐦 Willow goldfinch
- 🌼 Coast rhododendron
- 🌳 Western hemlock

West Virginia
- ⭐ Charleston
- 🐦 Cardinal
- 🌼 Rhododendron
- 🌳 Sugar maple

Wisconsin
- ⭐ Madison
- 🐦 Robin
- 🌼 Wood violet
- 🌳 Sugar maple

Wyoming
- ⭐ Cheyenne
- 🐦 Meadow lark
- 🌼 Indian paintbrush
- 🌳 Cottonwood

9

About the United States

There are four main parts of the U.S. called regions – the Northeast, South, Midwest, and West. Each region differs from the others in many ways, such as weather, animals, plants and trees, farming, industry, and places of interest. The West is the largest region, and the Northeast is the smallest.

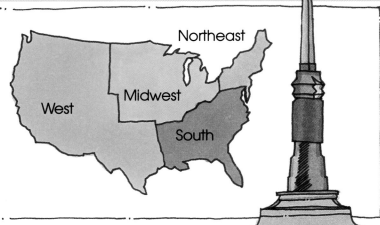

The Northeast

The many natural harbors, lakes, and rivers attracted settlers to this region. People from all over the world still arrive at its ports to begin a new life in the United States.

Summers are usually hot and damp, but the winters are quite cold.

New York Harbor

Most of the people of this region live in cities.

New York is the most crowded city in the United States. As many people visit it each year as live there. It is also one of the world's three major business centers.

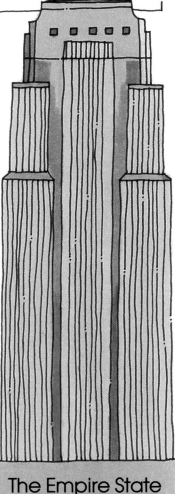

The Empire State Building is very popular with tourists.

There are many hills and mountain ranges.

Beavers, weasels, deer, and porcupines live in the forests.

10

The South

The sandy beaches of the South make it a good place for vacations. It is also a big farming area, producing tobacco, soybeans, cotton, and peanuts.

Walt Disney World in Orlando, Florida, is a giant amusement park.

Kentucky and Virginia are famous for breeding fine horses.

Nashville, Tennessee, is the national capital for country music.

Atlanta, Georgia, has one of the busiest airports in the country.

Traditional Southern dishes include cornbread, grits and gumbo.

Forty kinds of snake live in the Everglades National Park, Florida.

Alligators are found in the swamplands.

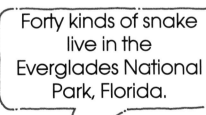

Skunks, opossums, and snakes live in the South.

The Midwest

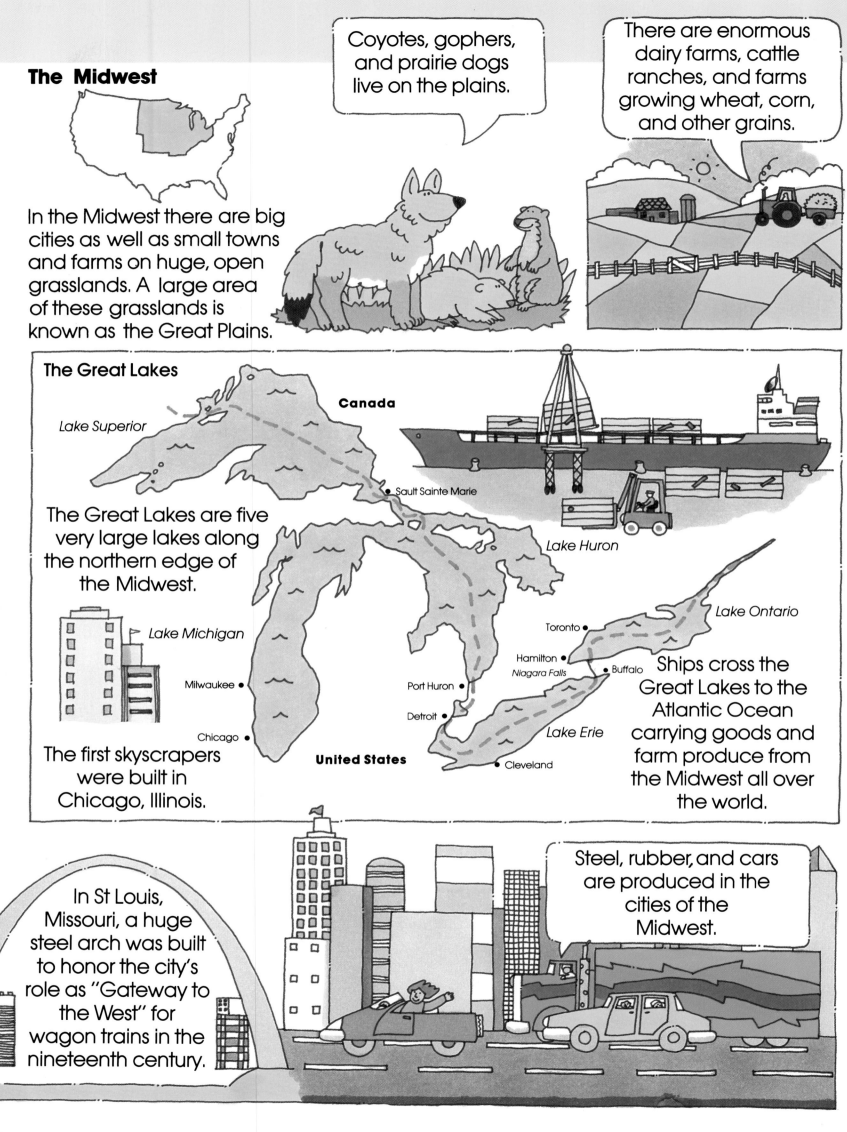

In the Midwest there are big cities as well as small towns and farms on huge, open grasslands. A large area of these grasslands is known as the Great Plains.

Coyotes, gophers, and prairie dogs live on the plains.

There are enormous dairy farms, cattle ranches, and farms growing wheat, corn, and other grains.

The Great Lakes

The Great Lakes are five very large lakes along the northern edge of the Midwest.

The first skyscrapers were built in Chicago, Illinois.

Canada

Lake Superior

Sault Sainte Marie

Lake Huron

Lake Michigan

Milwaukee

Chicago

Toronto

Hamilton

Niagara Falls

Buffalo

Port Huron

Detroit

Lake Ontario

Lake Erie

Cleveland

United States

Ships cross the Great Lakes to the Atlantic Ocean carrying goods and farm produce from the Midwest all over the world.

In St Louis, Missouri, a huge steel arch was built to honor the city's role as "Gateway to the West" for wagon trains in the nineteenth century.

Steel, rubber, and cars are produced in the cities of the Midwest.

The West

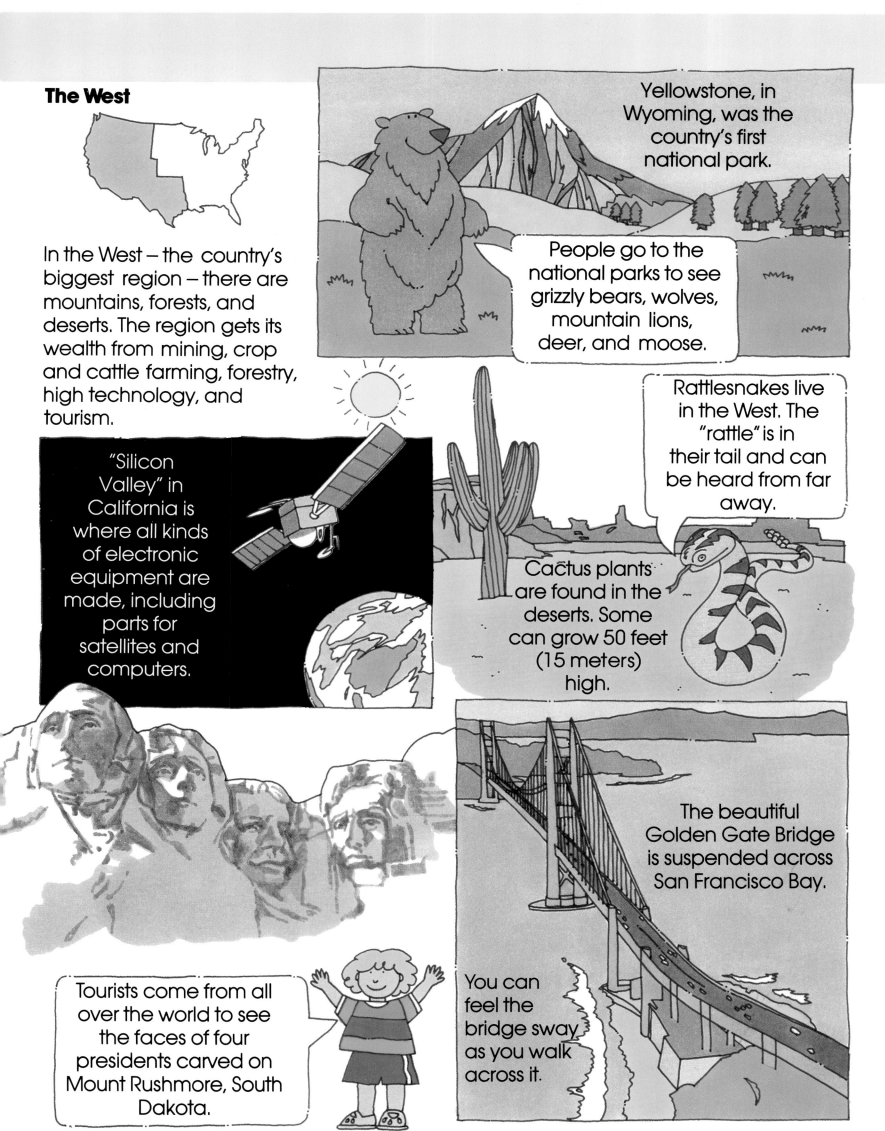

In the West – the country's biggest region – there are mountains, forests, and deserts. The region gets its wealth from mining, crop and cattle farming, forestry, high technology, and tourism.

Yellowstone, in Wyoming, was the country's first national park.

People go to the national parks to see grizzly bears, wolves, mountain lions, deer, and moose.

"Silicon Valley" in California is where all kinds of electronic equipment are made, including parts for satellites and computers.

Rattlesnakes live in the West. The "rattle" is in their tail and can be heard from far away.

Cactus plants are found in the deserts. Some can grow 50 feet (15 meters) high.

The beautiful Golden Gate Bridge is suspended across San Francisco Bay.

Tourists come from all over the world to see the faces of four presidents carved on Mount Rushmore, South Dakota.

You can feel the bridge sway as you walk across it.

North America

North America contains Canada, the United States of America, Mexico, and the countries of Central America. Canada is the second largest country in the world. The U.S. is the fourth largest and has fifty states.

The Canadian flag

Ice hockey is a very popular sport in Canada.

Skiing is popular in the Rocky mountains. The Rockies run from Canada, through the United States.

The U.S. produces more timber than any other country.

Canadian police are called Mounties. Some still ride horses, but most drive cars or motocycles nowadays.

Alaska (USA)

Yukon River

Alaskan Mountains

Fairbanks •

• Anchorage

Great Bear Lake

Mackenzie River

Great Slave Lake

Lake Athabasca

Rocky Mountains

Columbia River

Snake River

Coastal Mountains

Sierra Nevada

Colorado River

Vancouver •

Fact file

Highest mountain: Mount McKinley, Alaska, 20,322 ft (6,194 m).

Longest river: Mississippi River, U.S., 3,859 miles (6,212 km).

Largest lake: Lake Michigan, U.S., is the second longest in the world, 22,400 sq miles (58,016 sq km).

Weather: Canada and Alaska are colder than the rest of the U.S. and the West Indies.

Biggest city: New York, U.S. about 7 million people.

Number of people: Canada, about 26 million. U.S., about 249 million. Mexico, about 67 million. Costa Rica, about 2.5 million. Panama, about 2 million.

One of the world's most active volcanos, Mauna Loa, is on the island of Hawaii.

Hawaii (USA)

The Aztecs were a civilization in Mexico hundreds of years ago. Mexicans are proud of their Aztec ancestry.

Los Angeles •
San Diego •

The American flag

Pacific Ocean

Bananas, coffee, and sugar are grown in Central America.

The Mexican flag

KM	250	500	1000	1500	2000	2500	3000	3500	4000	4500	5000	5500	6000	6500
MILES		250	500	1000		1500		2000		2500		3000		3500	4000

Canadian Indians and Inuit were the first people to live in Canada.

Atlantic Ocean

The Statue of Liberty was given to Americans by the French. It stands in New York harbor.

Beavers live in the forests and woods of Canada.

Canada

Lake Winnipeg

The Great Lakes

Lake Superior

Montreal

St Lawrence River

Ottawa ■
Toronto

Minneapolis

Lake Huron

Lake Ontario

Boston

Lake Michigan

New York
Philadelphia

Chicago

Lake Erie

United States

Arkansas River

Ohio River

Appalachian Mountains

Atlanta

Dallas

Mississippi River

In the Caribbean Sea are thousands of islands called the West Indies, where it is sunny all year round.

Bermuda

New Orleans

Houston

Rio Grande

Gulf of Mexico

Miami

The Bahamas

Cuba

Mexico

Mexico City

The first rockets sent into space were launched from Cape Canaveral in Florida.

The West Indies

Virgin Islands

Dominican Republic

Antigua & Barbuda

Guadeloupe

St Kitts – Nevis

Dominica

Puerto Rico

Barbados

Martinique

Haiti

St Lucia

Tobago

St Vincent

Trinidad

Grenada

Jamaica

Hurricanes sometimes cause much damage in the West Indies.

Belize
Belmopan

Honduras

Guatemala

Tegucigalpa

Guatemala

San Salvador

Nicaragua

El Salvador

Managua

Central America

Costa Rica

San José

Panama

Panama

Some American Indians carve totem poles out of wood.

	7500		8000	8500	9000	9500	10,000	10,500	11,000	11,500	12,000	12,500	13,000	13,500	KM
4500		5000		5500		6000		6500		7000		7500		8000		MILES

South America

South America is the fourth largest continent. It is made up of 13 different countries. There are mountains and rain forests as well as plains and deserts. The weather ranges from very hot to very cold.

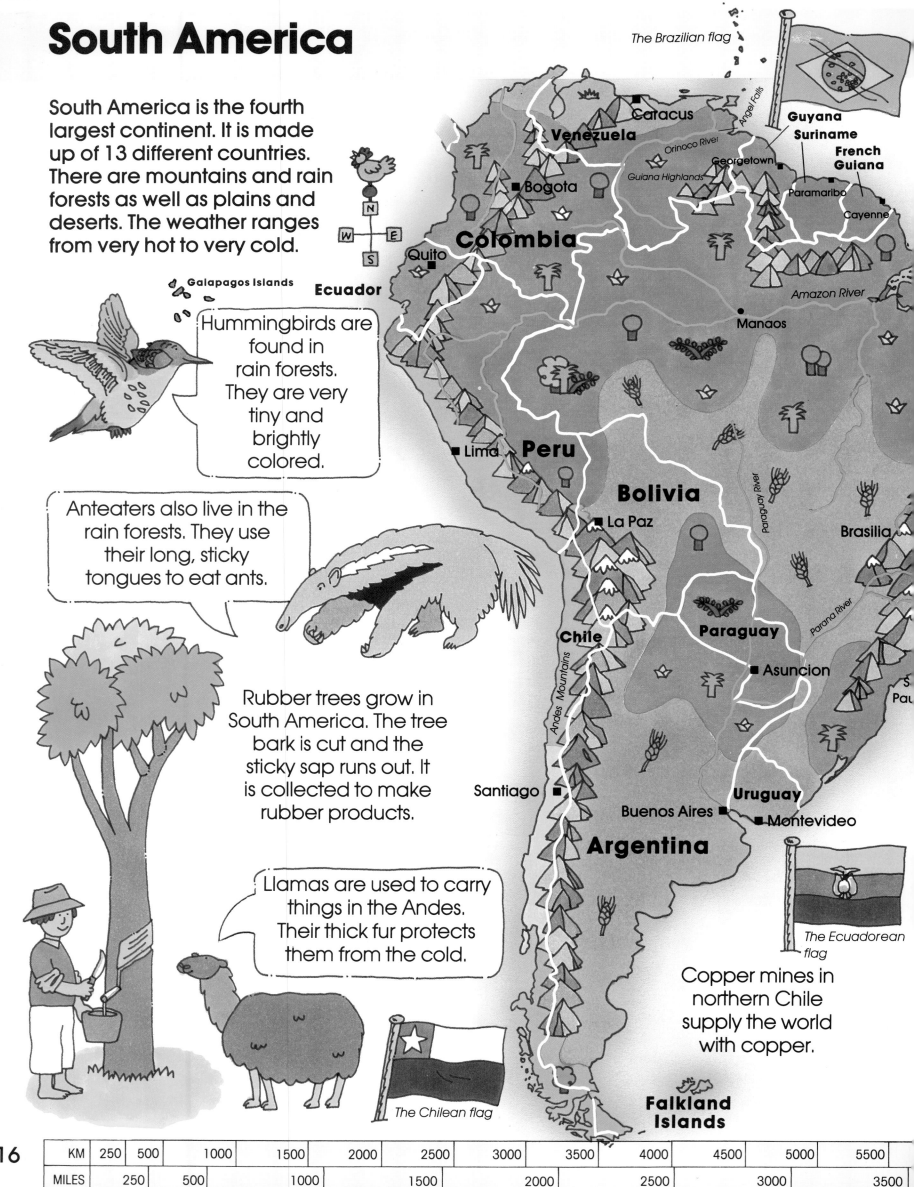

Hummingbirds are found in rain forests. They are very tiny and brightly colored.

Anteaters also live in the rain forests. They use their long, sticky tongues to eat ants.

Rubber trees grow in South America. The tree bark is cut and the sticky sap runs out. It is collected to make rubber products.

Llamas are used to carry things in the Andes. Their thick fur protects them from the cold.

Copper mines in northern Chile supply the world with copper.

The Brazilian flag

Galapagos Islands

Ecuador

Venezuela
Caracus
Orinoco River
Angel Falls
Guyana
Suriname
French Guiana
Georgetown
Guiana Highlands
Paramaribo
Cayenne

Colombia
Bogota
Quito

Amazon River
Manaos

Peru
Lima

Bolivia
La Paz

Paraguay River

Brasilia

Paraguay
Asuncion
Parana River

S Pau

Chile
Andes Mountains
Santiago

Uruguay
Buenos Aires
Montevideo

Argentina

The Ecuadorean flag

The Chilean flag

Falkland Islands

KM	250	500	1000	1500	2000	2500	3000	3500	4000	4500	5000	5500
MILES	250	500	1000	1500	2000	2500	3000	3500

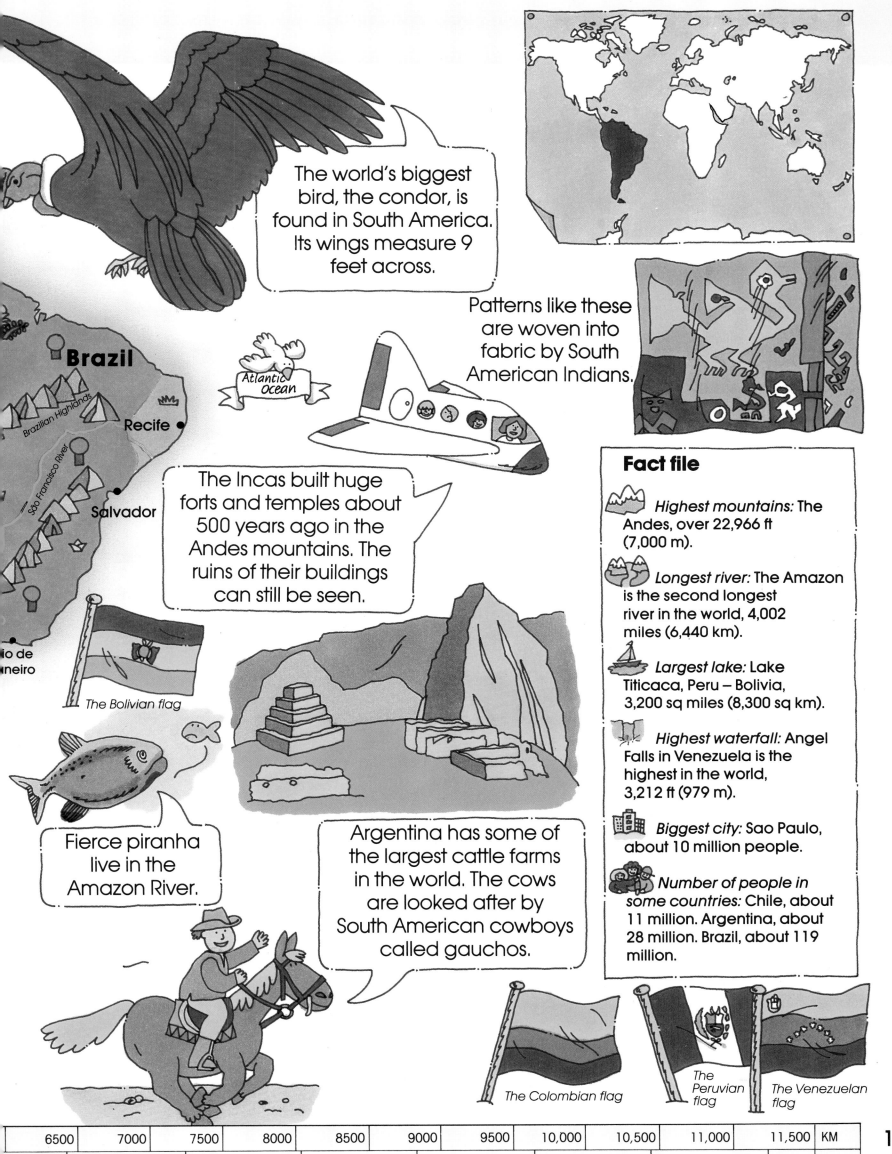

The world's biggest bird, the condor, is found in South America. Its wings measure 9 feet across.

Brazil

Atlantic Ocean

Brazilian Highlands

Recife

São Francisco River

Salvador

Patterns like these are woven into fabric by South American Indians.

The Incas built huge forts and temples about 500 years ago in the Andes mountains. The ruins of their buildings can still be seen.

Rio de Janeiro

The Bolivian flag

Fierce piranha live in the Amazon River.

Argentina has some of the largest cattle farms in the world. The cows are looked after by South American cowboys called gauchos.

Fact file

Highest mountains: The Andes, over 22,966 ft (7,000 m).

Longest river: The Amazon is the second longest river in the world, 4,002 miles (6,440 km).

Largest lake: Lake Titicaca, Peru – Bolivia, 3,200 sq miles (8,300 sq km).

Highest waterfall: Angel Falls in Venezuela is the highest in the world, 3,212 ft (979 m).

Biggest city: Sao Paulo, about 10 million people.

Number of people in some countries: Chile, about 11 million. Argentina, about 28 million. Brazil, about 119 million.

The Colombian flag

The Peruvian flag

The Venezuelan flag

6500	7000	7500	8000	8500	9000	9500	10,000	10,500	11,000	11,500	KM
4000		4500		5000		5500		6000		6500		7000	MILES

Northern Europe

These northern European countries are known as Scandinavia. Norway has over 150,000 islands along its coastline. The Norwegian coast is jagged, with deep inlets called fjords. Forests and lakes cover large areas of Scandinavia. Many bears and wolves used to live in the forests.

Workers travel to the oil rigs by helicopter.

Children here learn to ski almost as soon as they can walk!

There is oil under the sea bed. Oil rigs are used to pump the oil up to the surface.

The oil is used as fuel for cars and for heating buildings.

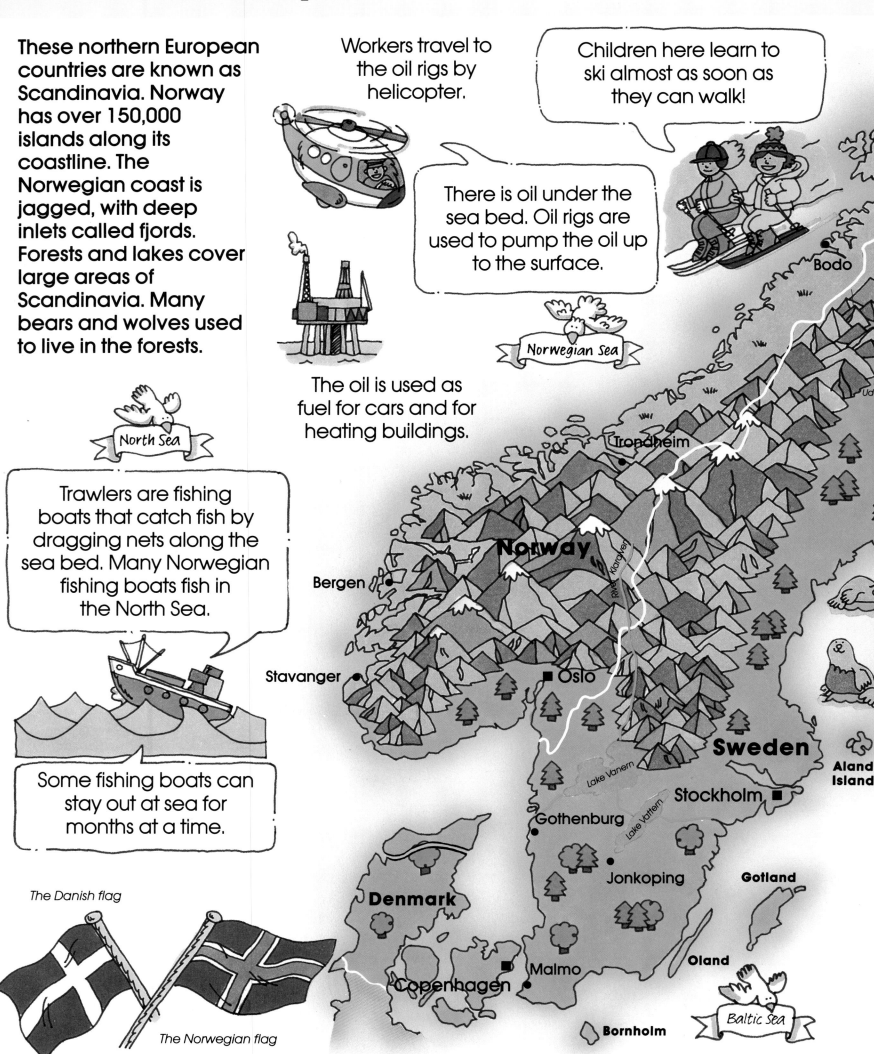

Norwegian Sea

North Sea

Trawlers are fishing boats that catch fish by dragging nets along the sea bed. Many Norwegian fishing boats fish in the North Sea.

Some fishing boats can stay out at sea for months at a time.

Bodo

Trondheim

River Klarglven

Norway

Bergen

Stavanger

Oslo

Sweden

Aland Islands

Lake Vanern

Stockholm

Gothenburg

Lake Vattern

Jonkoping

Gotland

The Danish flag

Denmark

Oland

Copenhagen

Malmo

Bornholm

Baltic Sea

The Norwegian flag

KM	250	500	1000
MILES	250	500	

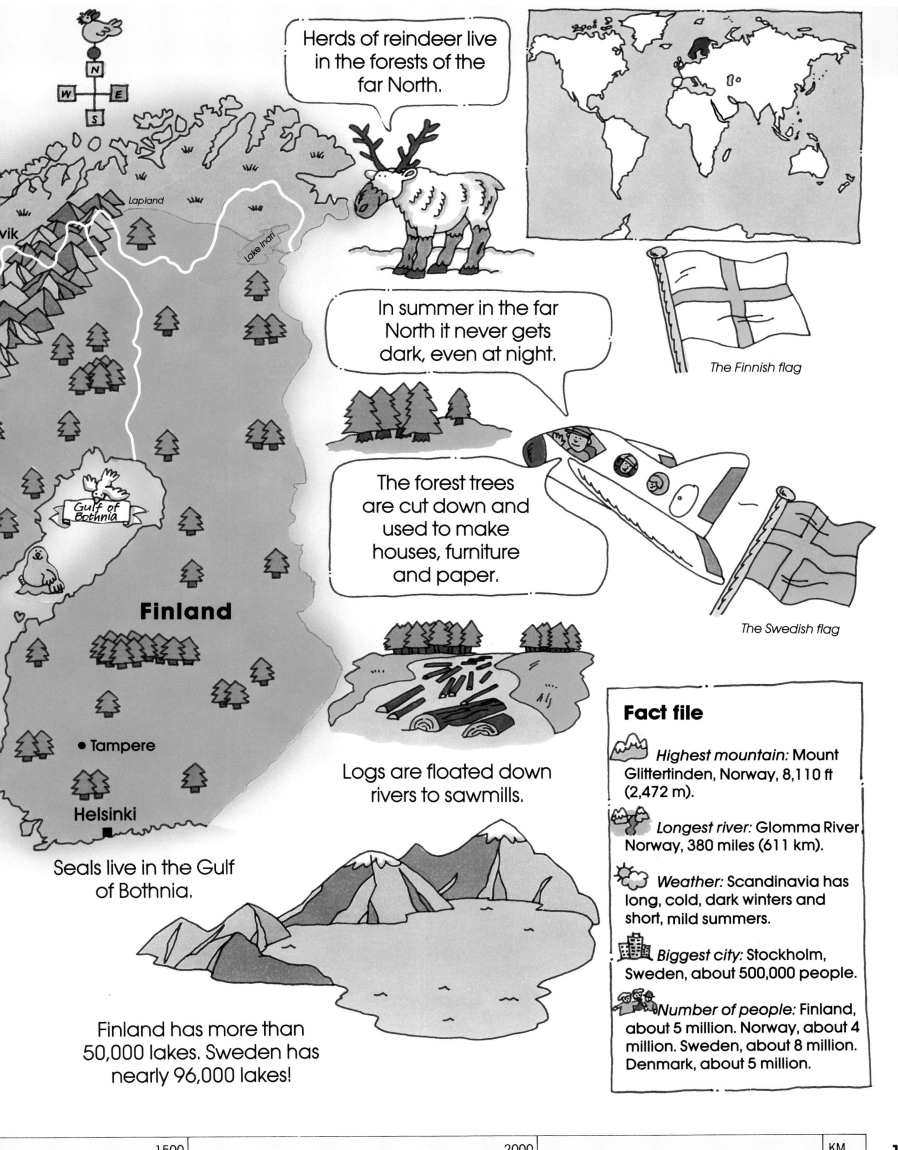

Herds of reindeer live in the forests of the far North.

In summer in the far North it never gets dark, even at night.

The forest trees are cut down and used to make houses, furniture and paper.

The Finnish flag

The Swedish flag

Lapland

Lake Inari

vik

Gulf of Bothnia

Finland

• Tampere

Helsinki

Seals live in the Gulf of Bothnia.

Logs are floated down rivers to sawmills.

Finland has more than 50,000 lakes. Sweden has nearly 96,000 lakes!

Fact file

Highest mountain: Mount Glittertinden, Norway, 8,110 ft (2,472 m).

Longest river: Glomma River, Norway, 380 miles (611 km).

Weather: Scandinavia has long, cold, dark winters and short, mild summers.

Biggest city: Stockholm, Sweden, about 500,000 people.

Number of people: Finland, about 5 million. Norway, about 4 million. Sweden, about 8 million. Denmark, about 5 million.

| 1500 | | 2000 | | KM |
| 1000 | | | 1500 | | MILES |

Britain and Central Europe

On this map you can see fourteen different countries. Some, like Luxembourg, are tiny. Others, such as France, are large. There are very high mountains, called the Alps, in Switzerland and Austria, but most of the rest of Europe is flatter. The flat land is very good for farming.

Britain used to be joined to the rest of Europe. It became an island a long time ago when sea levels rose.

Northern Ireland

Ireland is known as the Emerald Isle because of its beautiful green hills and fields.

The British Crown Jewels are kept safely locked in the Tower of London.

More than 300 different kinds of cheese are made in France.

Grapes are grown in parts of France and Germany. They are used to make wine.

The Eiffel Tower is in Paris, the capital of France.

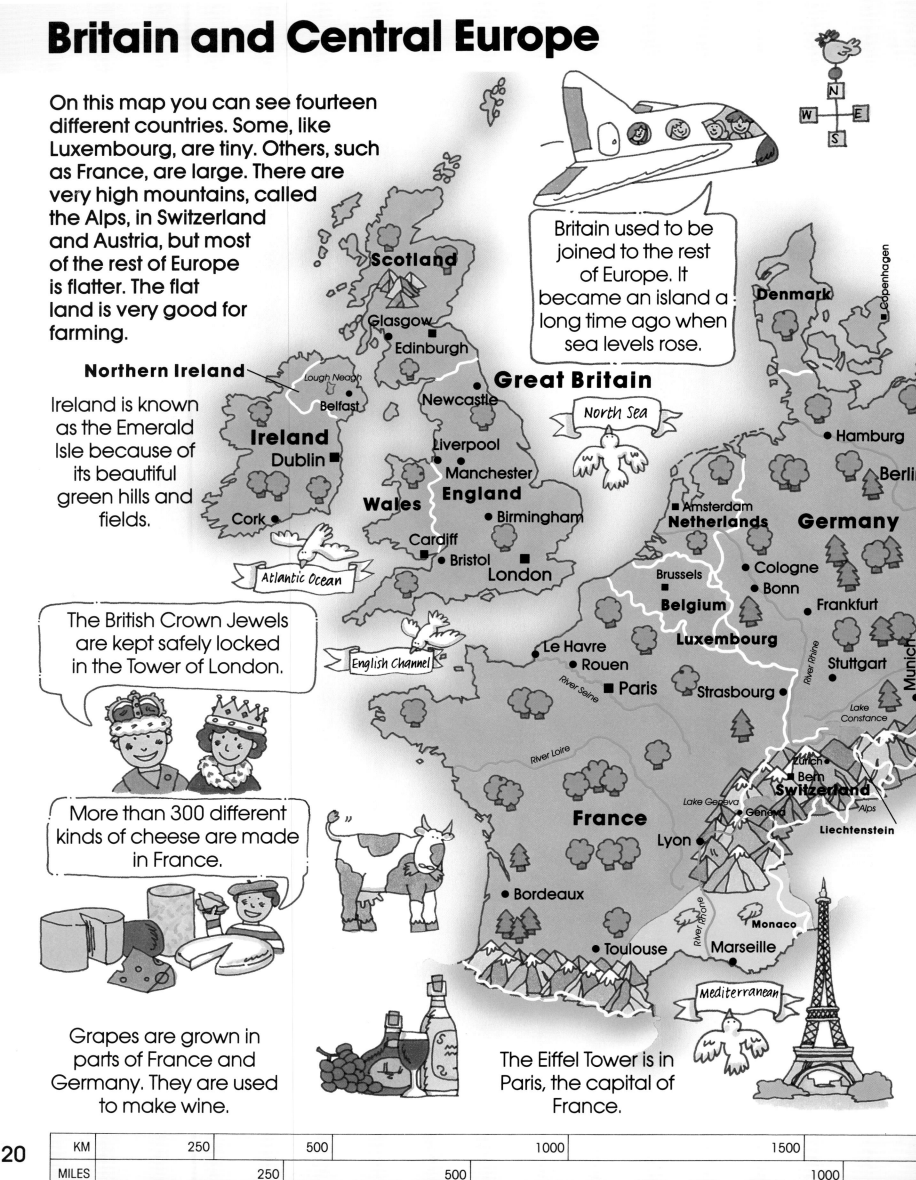

Scotland
Glasgow
Edinburgh
Lough Neagh
Belfast
Great Britain
Newcastle
North Sea
Ireland
Dublin
Liverpool
Manchester
England
Wales
Cork
Birmingham
Cardiff
Bristol
London
Atlantic Ocean
English Channel
Le Havre
Rouen
River Seine
Paris
France
River Loire
Bordeaux
Toulouse
River Rhône
Marseille
Mediterranean
Lyon
Denmark
Copenhagen
Hamburg
Berlin
Amsterdam
Netherlands
Germany
Brussels
Cologne
Bonn
Belgium
Frankfurt
Luxembourg
River Rhine
Stuttgart
Munich
Strasbourg
Lake Constance
Zürich
Bern
Switzerland
Lake Geneva
Geneva
Alps
Liechtenstein
Monaco

KM		250		500			1000			1500	
MILES			250			500				1000	

The Netherlands are so flat that the sea can flood in. Sea walls protect the land and windmills pump water away. Many Dutch farmers grow flowers.

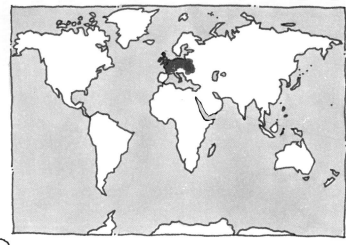

Germany, France, and Britain have big factories making many things from cars to computers.

The Swiss flag *The British Union Jack* *The French flag*

The German flag *The Austrian flag*

Gdansk ●

River Vistula

■ Warsaw

● Poznan

Poland

River Oder

● Wroclaw

River Elbe

● Krakow

Carpathians

ague ■

Czechoslovakia

Vienna ■

■ Budapest

● Cluj-Napoca

Hungary

Romania

Constanta
●

Salzburg

Timisoara ●

Bucharest ■

River Danube

Austria

Bulgaria

Skiing is a popular sport in the mountains.

■ Sofia

There are many fairytale castles built along the banks of the Rhine River in Germany.

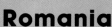

Fact file

Highest mountain: Mont Blanc, France, 15,771 ft (4,807 m).

Longest river: The Danube, 1,755 miles (2,824 km).

Weather: Most of this part of Europe has mild winters and cool summers. Rain falls all year round. Snow falls on high land in winter.

Biggest city: Paris, France, about 10 million people.

Number of people in some European countries: France, about 55 million. Great Britain (England, Scotland, and Wales), about 55 million. Germany, about 78 million. Netherlands, about 15 million. Luxembourg, about 366,000.

Mediterranean Europe

The countries around the Mediterranean Sea are sunny all year. Olives, fruit, and vegetables are grown in all these countries. Many people go to the Mediterranean for vacations. In parts of Spain and Italy there are high mountains where people ski in the winter.

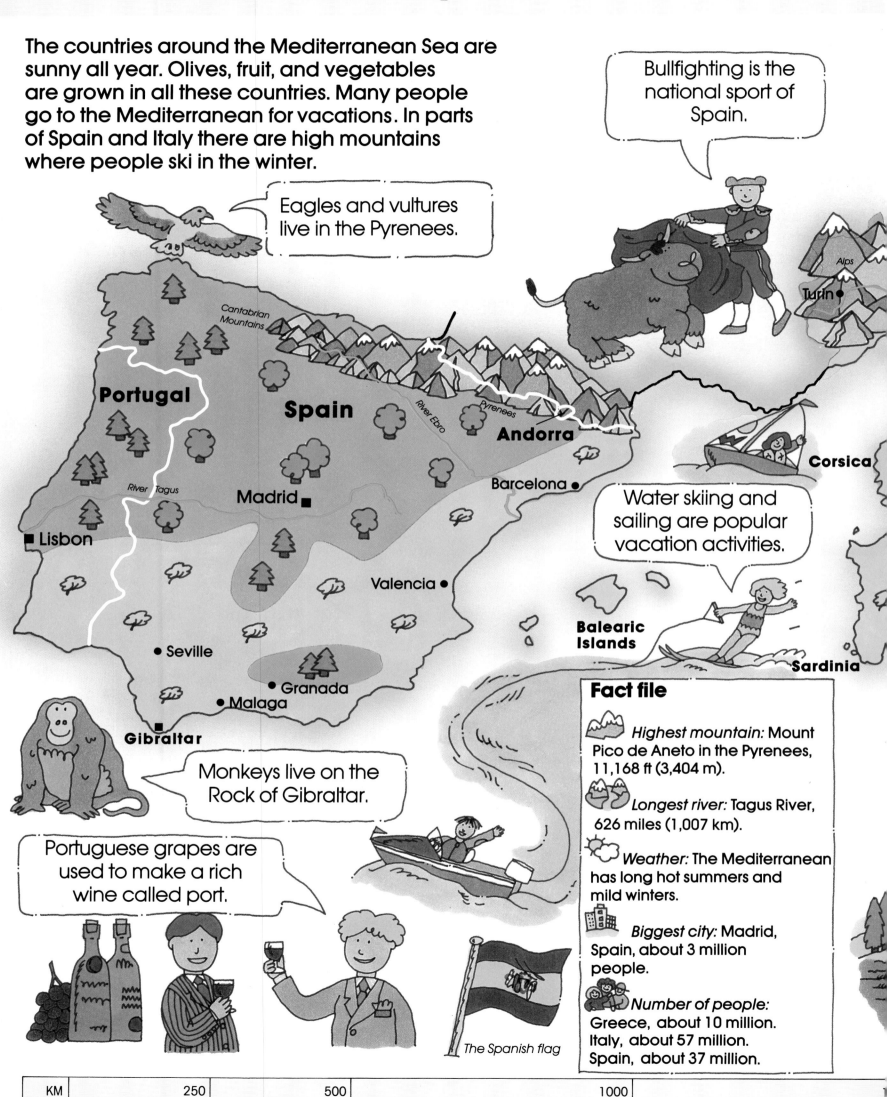

Bullfighting is the national sport of Spain.

Eagles and vultures live in the Pyrenees.

Alps

Turin

Cantabrian Mountains

Portugal

Spain

River Ebro

Pyrenees

Andorra

Barcelona

Corsica

River Tagus

Madrid

Water skiing and sailing are popular vacation activities.

Lisbon

Valencia

Balearic Islands

Sardinia

Seville

Granada

Malaga

Gibraltar

Monkeys live on the Rock of Gibraltar.

Portuguese grapes are used to make a rich wine called port.

The Spanish flag

Fact file

Highest mountain: Mount Pico de Aneto in the Pyrenees, 11,168 ft (3,404 m).

Longest river: Tagus River, 626 miles (1,007 km).

Weather: The Mediterranean has long hot summers and mild winters.

Biggest city: Madrid, Spain, about 3 million people.

Number of people: Greece, about 10 million. Italy, about 57 million. Spain, about 37 million.

| KM | | 250 | | 500 | | | 1000 | |
| MILES | | | 250 | | 500 | | | |

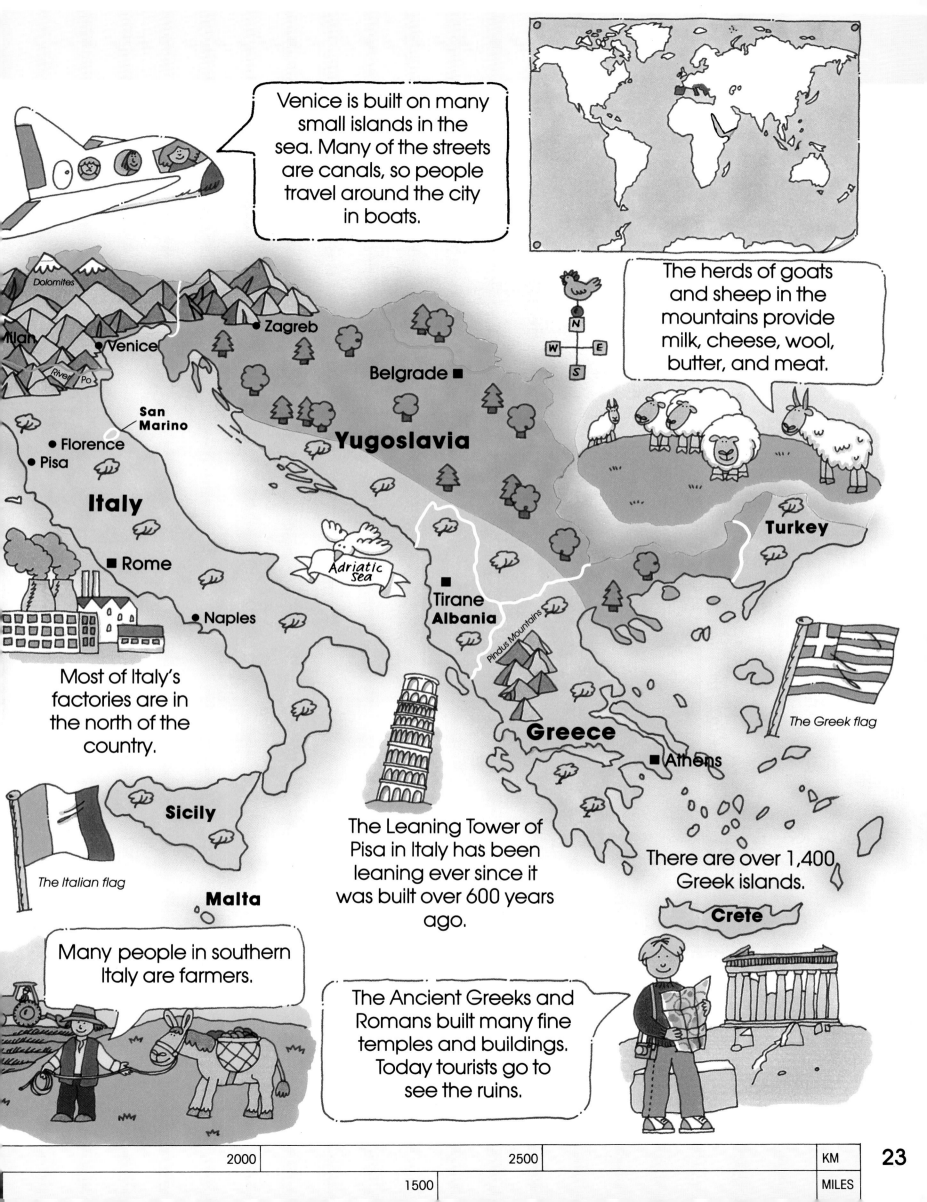

Venice is built on many small islands in the sea. Many of the streets are canals, so people travel around the city in boats.

The herds of goats and sheep in the mountains provide milk, cheese, wool, butter, and meat.

Dolomites

Milan

Venice

River Po

Zagreb

San Marino

Belgrade ■

Yugoslavia

• Florence

• Pisa

Italy

■ Rome

Adriatic Sea

Turkey

Tirane
Albania

Pindus Mountains

• Naples

Most of Italy's factories are in the north of the country.

The Greek flag

Greece

The Leaning Tower of Pisa in Italy has been leaning ever since it was built over 600 years ago.

■ Athens

Sicily

There are over 1,400 Greek islands.

The Italian flag

Malta

Crete

Many people in southern Italy are farmers.

The Ancient Greeks and Romans built many fine temples and buildings. Today tourists go to see the ruins.

Africa

Africa is the second largest continent in the world. It is split up into lots of different countries. Most of Africa is covered in grassland and desert. Some of the tropical rain forests in Africa have been chopped down to build villages and farms.

All sorts of wild animals are kept in huge safari parks so that they can be protected from danger. Tourists visit the parks.

The African elephant is the largest land animal in the world. Its ear is the same shape as the continent of Africa.

Diamonds and gold are mined in South Africa.

The Chad flag

The Nigerian flag

Madeira Island (Portugal)

Canary Islands (Spain)

Cape Verde Islands

Rabat
Morocco
Atlas Mountains
Western Sahara
Mauritania
Nouakchott
Dakar
Senegal
Banjul
Gambia
Bissau
Guinea-Bissau
Guinea
Conakry
Freetown
Sierra Leone
Monrovia
Liberia

Algiers
Tunis
Tunisia
Tripoli
Algeria
Libya
Mali
River Niger
Bamako
Burkina Faso
Ouagadougou
Niamey
Niger
Hoggar Mountains
Tibesti Mountains
Chad
Lake Chad
N'Djamena
Sud

Benin
Togo
Nigeria
Ghana
Lagos
Abidjan
Ivory Coast
Accra
Lomé
Porto-Novo

Cameroon
Bangui
Central African Republic
Equatorial Guinea
Libreville
Yaoundé
Congo
Gabon
Brazzaville
Kinshasa
Zaire
Rwan
Buru
River Zaire

Angola
Luanda
Atlantic Ocean
Angola
Zambi
Lusake
Zambezi River

Namibia
Windhoek
Botswana
Gaborone
Pretoria
Johannesburg
Drakensberg Mountains
Orange River
South Africa
Cape Town
Leso
Ma

24

KM	250	500	1000	1500	2000	2500	3000	3500	4000	4500	5000	5500	6000	6500
MILES		250	500	1000		1500		2000		2500		3000		3500	4000

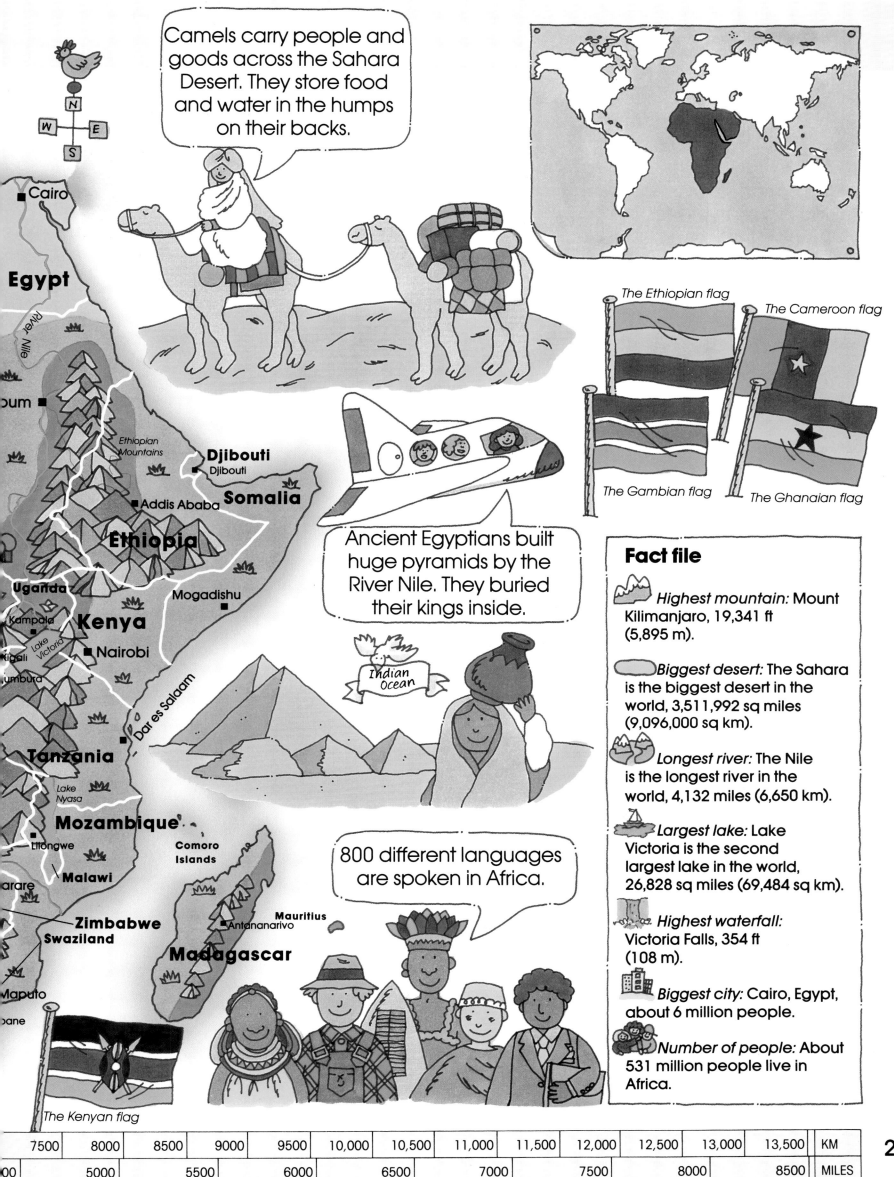

Camels carry people and goods across the Sahara Desert. They store food and water in the humps on their backs.

Ancient Egyptians built huge pyramids by the River Nile. They buried their kings inside.

800 different languages are spoken in Africa.

The Ethiopian flag

The Cameroon flag

The Gambian flag

The Ghanaian flag

Egypt

Cairo

River Nile

um

Ethiopian Mountains

Djibouti
Djibouti

Somalia

Addis Ababa

Ethiopia

Uganda

Mogadishu

Kampala

Kenya

Lake Victoria

Kigali

Nairobi

umbura

Dar es Salaam

Indian Ocean

Tanzania

Lake Nyasa

Mozambique

Litongwe

Comoro Islands

Malawi

arare

Mauritius

Zimbabwe
Antananarivo

Swaziland

Madagascar

Maputo

ane

The Kenyan flag

Fact file

Highest mountain: Mount Kilimanjaro, 19,341 ft (5,895 m).

Biggest desert: The Sahara is the biggest desert in the world, 3,511,992 sq miles (9,096,000 sq km).

Longest river: The Nile is the longest river in the world, 4,132 miles (6,650 km).

Largest lake: Lake Victoria is the second largest lake in the world, 26,828 sq miles (69,484 sq km).

Highest waterfall: Victoria Falls, 354 ft (108 m).

Biggest city: Cairo, Egypt, about 6 million people.

Number of people: About 531 million people live in Africa.

	7500	8000	8500	9000	9500	10,000	10,500	11,000	11,500	12,000	12,500	13,000	13,500	KM
00	5000		5500		6000		6500		7000		7500		8000		8500	MILES

U.S.S.R.

In 1991 the U.S.S.R. (the Soviet Union) began to split into several separate countries. Estonia, Lithuania, and Latvia were the first to be recognized by the rest of the world. Many changes are still taking place in this region.

The north is freezing cold, but the deserts in the south are burning hot. In between there are forests and farmlands.

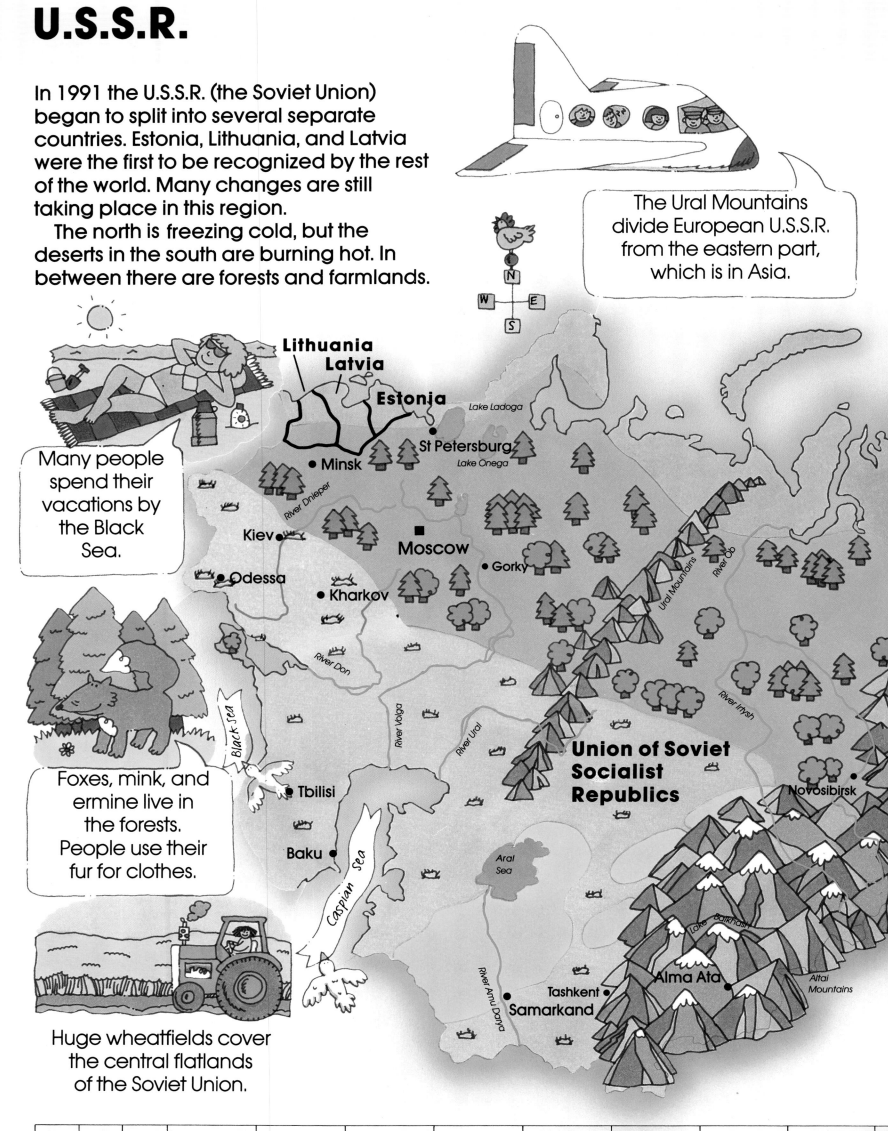

The Ural Mountains divide European U.S.S.R. from the eastern part, which is in Asia.

Many people spend their vacations by the Black Sea.

Foxes, mink, and ermine live in the forests. People use their fur for clothes.

Huge wheatfields cover the central flatlands of the Soviet Union.

Lithuania
Latvia
Estonia
Lake Ladoga
St Petersburg
Lake Onega
Minsk
River Dnieper
Kiev
Moscow
Gorky
Ural Mountains
River Ob
Odessa
Kharkov
River Don
River Irtysh
River Volga
River Ural
Black Sea
Union of Soviet Socialist Republics
Tbilisi
Novosibirsk
Baku
Aral Sea
Caspian Sea
Lake Balkhash
Alma Ata
Altai Mountains
River Amu Darya
Tashkent
Samarkand

KM	250	500	1000	1500	2000	2500	3000	3500	4000	4500
MILES		250	500	1000	1500	2000		2500		

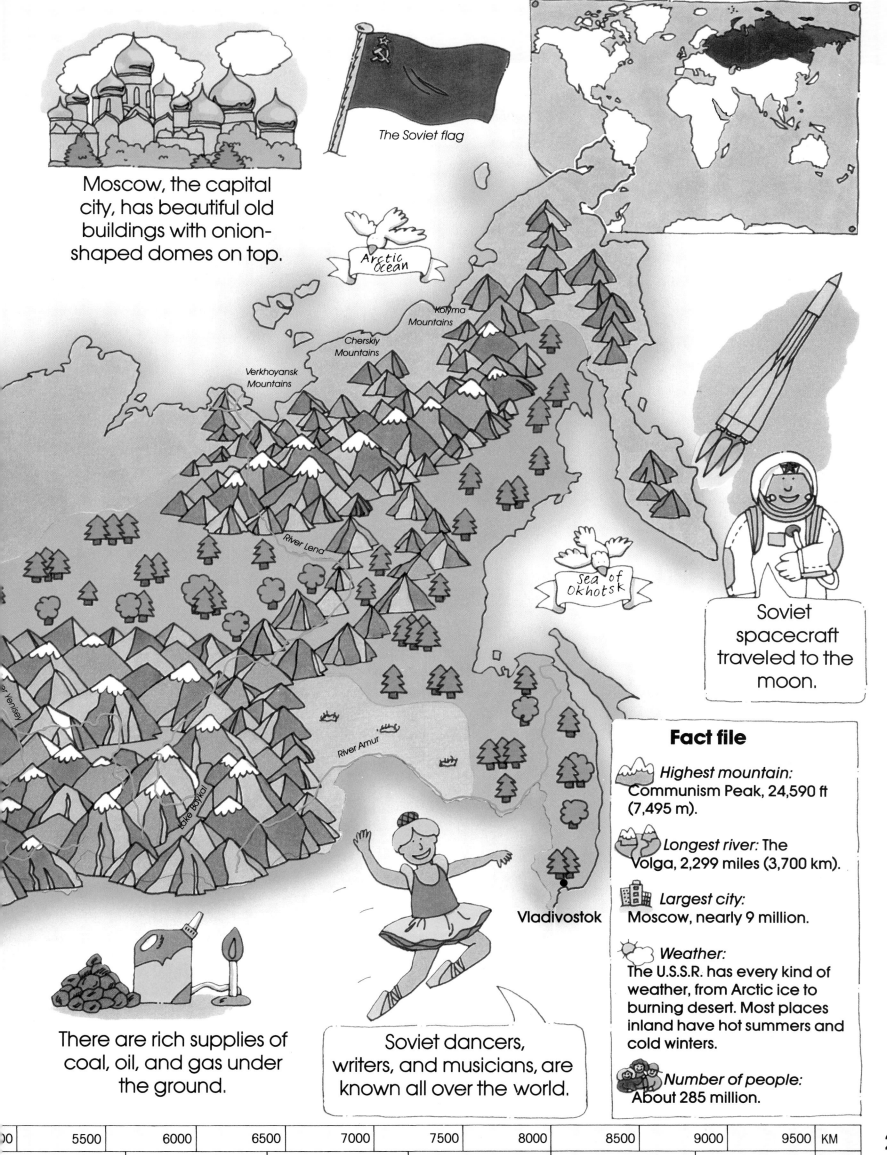

Moscow, the capital city, has beautiful old buildings with onion-shaped domes on top.

The Soviet flag

Arctic Ocean

Kolyma Mountains

Cherskiy Mountains

Verkhoyansk Mountains

River Lena

Sea of Okhotsk

River Yenisey

River Amur

Lake Baykal

Vladivostok

Soviet spacecraft traveled to the moon.

Fact file

Highest mountain: Communism Peak, 24,590 ft (7,495 m).

Longest river: The Volga, 2,299 miles (3,700 km).

Largest city: Moscow, nearly 9 million.

Weather: The U.S.S.R. has every kind of weather, from Arctic ice to burning desert. Most places inland have hot summers and cold winters.

Number of people: About 285 million.

There are rich supplies of coal, oil, and gas under the ground.

Soviet dancers, writers, and musicians, are known all over the world.

	5500	6000	6500	7000	7500	8000	8500	9000	9500	KM
		3500		4000		4500		5000		5500		MILES

The Middle East

Most of the Middle East is either mountainous or hot, sandy desert. Some of the countries have a great deal of valuable oil under the ground. The oil is pumped up to the surface at oil wells. It is then sold to other countries for use as gasoline and other kinds of fuel.

The Israeli flag

Black Sea

The United Arab Emirates flag

Jerusalem, in Israel, is a holy city for Jews, Christians, and Muslims.

Every year millions of Muslims make a special journey to their holy city of Mecca, in Saudi Arabia.

The desert in the south of Saudi Arabia covers almost a quarter of the country. It is the largest stretch of sand in the world.

Istanbul
Ankara
Turkey
Taurus Mountains
River Euphrates
River Tigris
Cyprus
Nicosia
Mediterranean Sea
Syria
Damascus
Baghdad
Lebanon
Beirut
Iraq
Israel
Tel Aviv
Jerusalem
Amman
Basra
Jordan
Kuwait City
Kuwait
Bahrain
Al-Manama
Doh
Saudi Arabia
Riyadh
Mecca
N
W E
S
Red Sea
South Yemen
Sap'a
Aden

KM	250	500		1000	1500	2000	2500
MILES		250	500		1000		1500

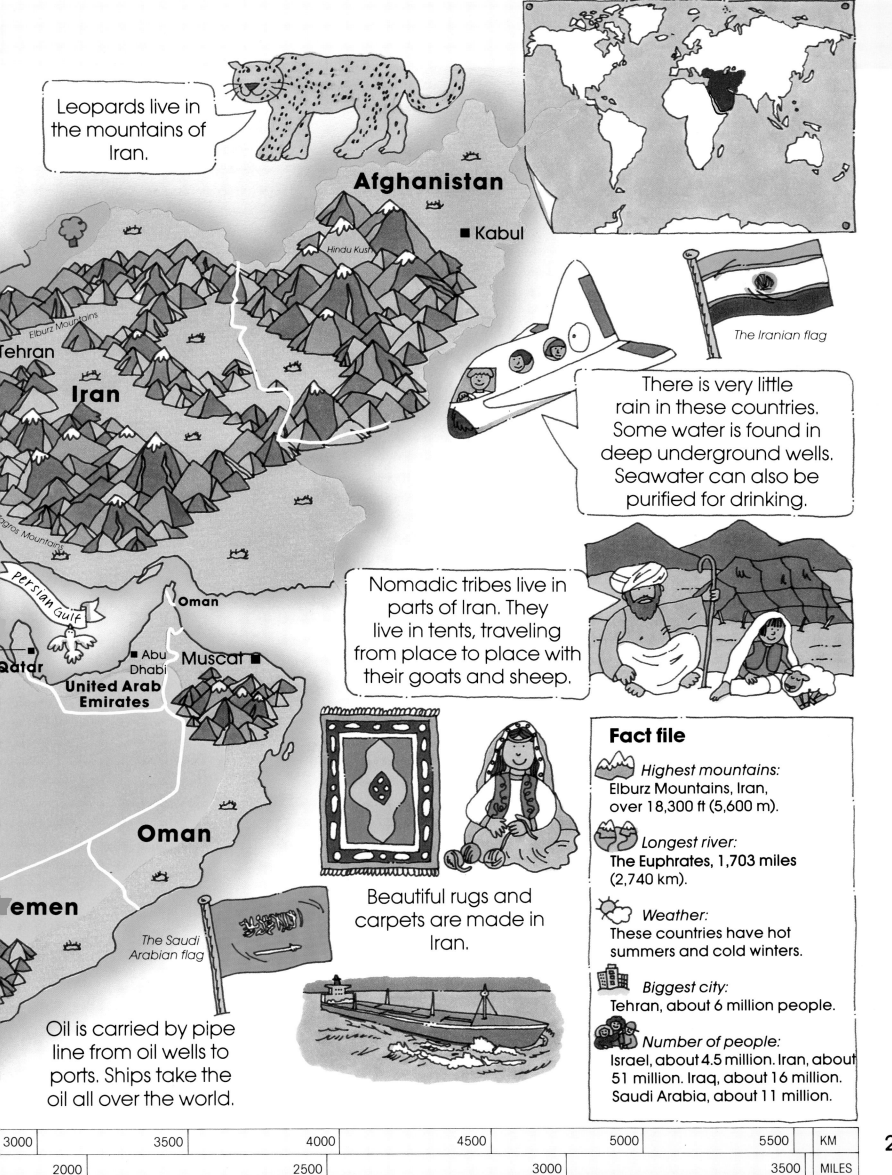

Leopards live in the mountains of Iran.

Afghanistan

■ Kabul

Hindu Kush

Elburz Mountains

Tehran

Iran

Zagros Mountains

Persian Gulf

Oman

Qatar

■ Abu Dhabi

Muscat ■

United Arab Emirates

Oman

Yemen

The Saudi Arabian flag

Oil is carried by pipe line from oil wells to ports. Ships take the oil all over the world.

The Iranian flag

There is very little rain in these countries. Some water is found in deep underground wells. Seawater can also be purified for drinking.

Nomadic tribes live in parts of Iran. They live in tents, traveling from place to place with their goats and sheep.

Beautiful rugs and carpets are made in Iran.

Fact file

Highest mountains:
Elburz Mountains, Iran, over 18,300 ft (5,600 m).

Longest river:
The Euphrates, 1,703 miles (2,740 km).

Weather:
These countries have hot summers and cold winters.

Biggest city:
Tehran, about 6 million people.

Number of people:
Israel, about 4.5 million. Iran, about 51 million. Iraq, about 16 million. Saudi Arabia, about 11 million.

| 3000 | 3500 | 4000 | 4500 | 5000 | 5500 | KM |
| 2000 | 2500 | 3000 | 3500 | MILES |

South Asia

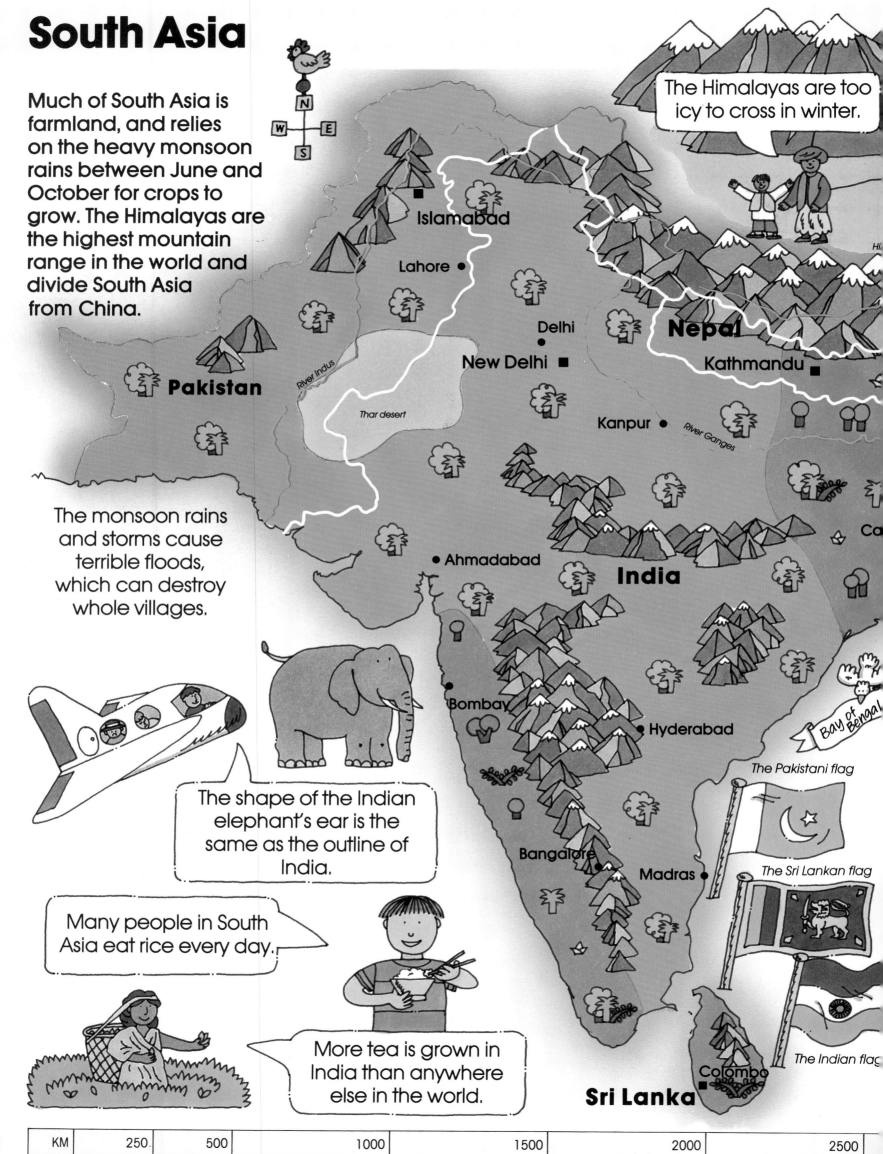

Much of South Asia is farmland, and relies on the heavy monsoon rains between June and October for crops to grow. The Himalayas are the highest mountain range in the world and divide South Asia from China.

The monsoon rains and storms cause terrible floods, which can destroy whole villages.

The Himalayas are too icy to cross in winter.

The shape of the Indian elephant's ear is the same as the outline of India.

Many people in South Asia eat rice every day.

More tea is grown in India than anywhere else in the world.

Islamabad

Lahore •

Pakistan

River Indus

Thar desert

Delhi
•
New Delhi ■

Nepal

Kathmandu ■

Kanpur •
River Ganges

• Ahmadabad

India

Bombay

Hyderabad •

Bay of Bengal

The Pakistani flag

Bangalore
•

Madras •

The Sri Lankan flag

Colombo ■

Sri Lanka

The Indian flag

	KM	250	500		1000		1500		2000		2500
	MILES		250		500			1000			1500

Ponies, yaks, and even sheep are used to carry goods across the Himalayas.

Thimbu
Bhutan
River Brahmaputra
Bangladesh
Dhaka

Elephants and tigers live on the lower slopes of the Himalayas and in the swamps of the Ganges River.

India is the second most crowded country in the world.

Fact file

Highest mountain: Mount Everest, 29,029 ft (8,848 m).

Longest river: Ganges-Brahmaputra, 1,802 miles (2,900 km).

Weather: It is very cold in the mountains, but hot most of the year elsewhere.

Biggest city: Calcutta, about 9 million people.

Number of people in some countries:
Nepal, about 18 million.
Bangladesh, about 110 million.
Bhutan, about 1.5 million.
India, about 836 million.
Sri Lanka, about 17 million.
Pakistan, about 118 million.

Cows are sacred animals in India. They are not kept in fields but are allowed to graze where they like.

Cotton plants produce threads that are made into cotton fabric. It can be painted or dyed and made into clothes.

The Taj Mahal, near Agra in northern India, is often called the most beautiful building in the world.

| 3000 | | 3500 | | 4000 | | 4500 | | 5000 | | KM |
| 2000 | | | 2500 | | | 3000 | | | MILES |

Southeast Asia and Pacific Islands

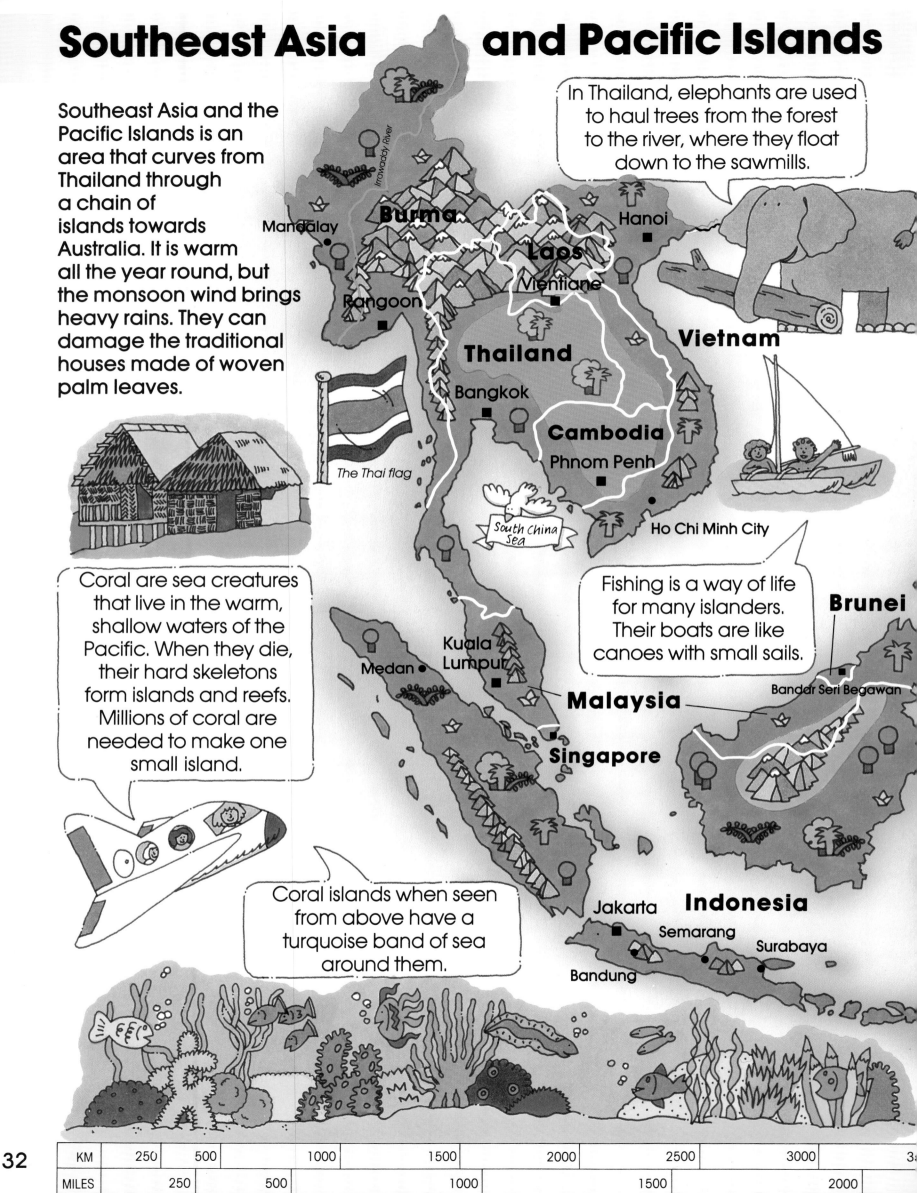

Southeast Asia and the Pacific Islands is an area that curves from Thailand through a chain of islands towards Australia. It is warm all the year round, but the monsoon wind brings heavy rains. They can damage the traditional houses made of woven palm leaves.

In Thailand, elephants are used to haul trees from the forest to the river, where they float down to the sawmills.

Coral are sea creatures that live in the warm, shallow waters of the Pacific. When they die, their hard skeletons form islands and reefs. Millions of coral are needed to make one small island.

Fishing is a way of life for many islanders. Their boats are like canoes with small sails.

Coral islands when seen from above have a turquoise band of sea around them.

The Thai flag

Irrawaddy River

Burma
Mandalay
Rangoon
Hanoi
Laos
Vientiane
Vietnam
Thailand
Bangkok
Cambodia
Phnom Penh
South China Sea
Ho Chi Minh City
Kuala Lumpur
Medan
Malaysia
Brunei
Bandar Seri Begawan
Singapore
Jakarta
Indonesia
Semarang
Surabaya
Bandung

| KM | 250 | 500 | | 1000 | 1500 | 2000 | 2500 | 3000 | 3 |
| MILES | | 250 | 500 | | 1000 | | 1500 | | 2000 |

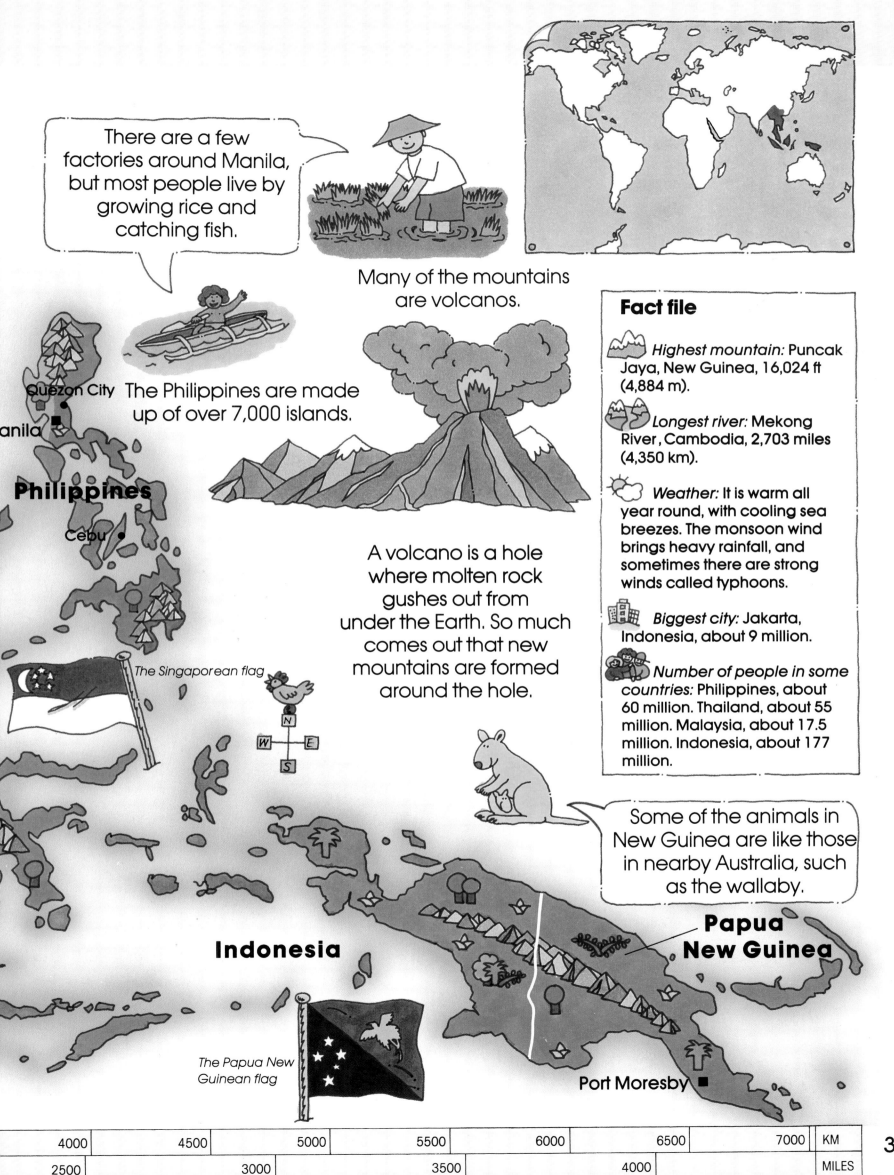

There are a few factories around Manila, but most people live by growing rice and catching fish.

Many of the mountains are volcanos.

The Philippines are made up of over 7,000 islands.

Quezon City

Manila

Philippines

Cebu

The Singaporean flag

N
W   E
S

A volcano is a hole where molten rock gushes out from under the Earth. So much comes out that new mountains are formed around the hole.

Fact file

Highest mountain: Puncak Jaya, New Guinea, 16,024 ft (4,884 m).

Longest river: Mekong River, Cambodia, 2,703 miles (4,350 km).

Weather: It is warm all year round, with cooling sea breezes. The monsoon wind brings heavy rainfall, and sometimes there are strong winds called typhoons.

Biggest city: Jakarta, Indonesia, about 9 million.

Number of people in some countries: Philippines, about 60 million. Thailand, about 55 million. Malaysia, about 17.5 million. Indonesia, about 177 million.

Some of the animals in New Guinea are like those in nearby Australia, such as the wallaby.

Indonesia

Papua New Guinea

The Papua New Guinean flag

Port Moresby

| 4000 | 4500 | 5000 | 5500 | 6000 | 6500 | 7000 | KM |
| 2500 | | 3000 | | 3500 | 4000 | | MILES |

East Asia

China is the third largest country in the world. Japan is much smaller, about the same size as Britain, but it is the richest country in Asia.

Chinese temples and pagodas have tiled roofs that curl up at the corners.

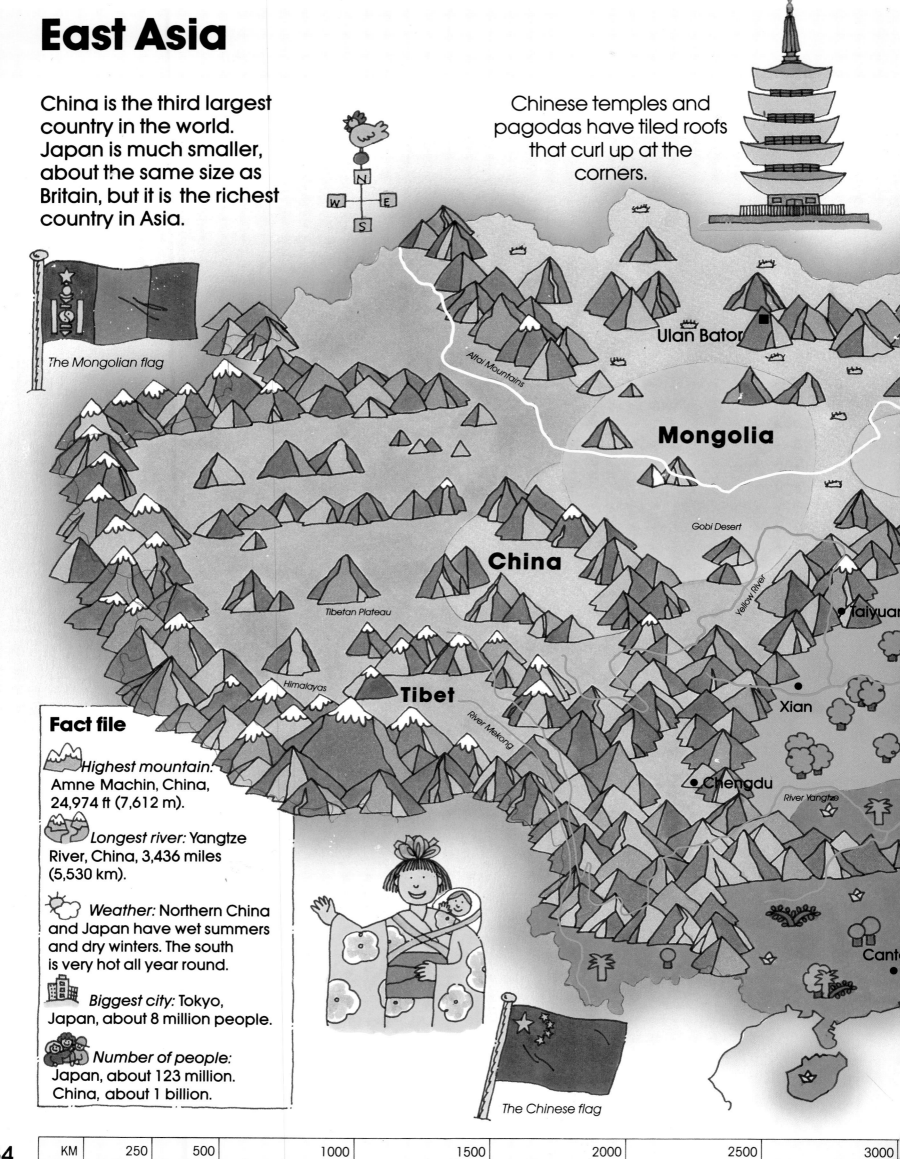

The Mongolian flag

Mongolia

Ulan Bator

Altai Mountains

Gobi Desert

Yellow River

China

Taiyuan

Tibetan Plateau

Xian

Himalayas

Tibet

River Mekong

Chengdu

River Yangtze

Cant

Fact file

Highest mountain: Amne Machin, China, 24,974 ft (7,612 m).

Longest river: Yangtze River, China, 3,436 miles (5,530 km).

Weather: Northern China and Japan have wet summers and dry winters. The south is very hot all year round.

Biggest city: Tokyo, Japan, about 8 million people.

Number of people: Japan, about 123 million. China, about 1 billion.

The Chinese flag

KM		250	500		1000		1500		2000		2500		3000
MILES			250	500			1000			1500			

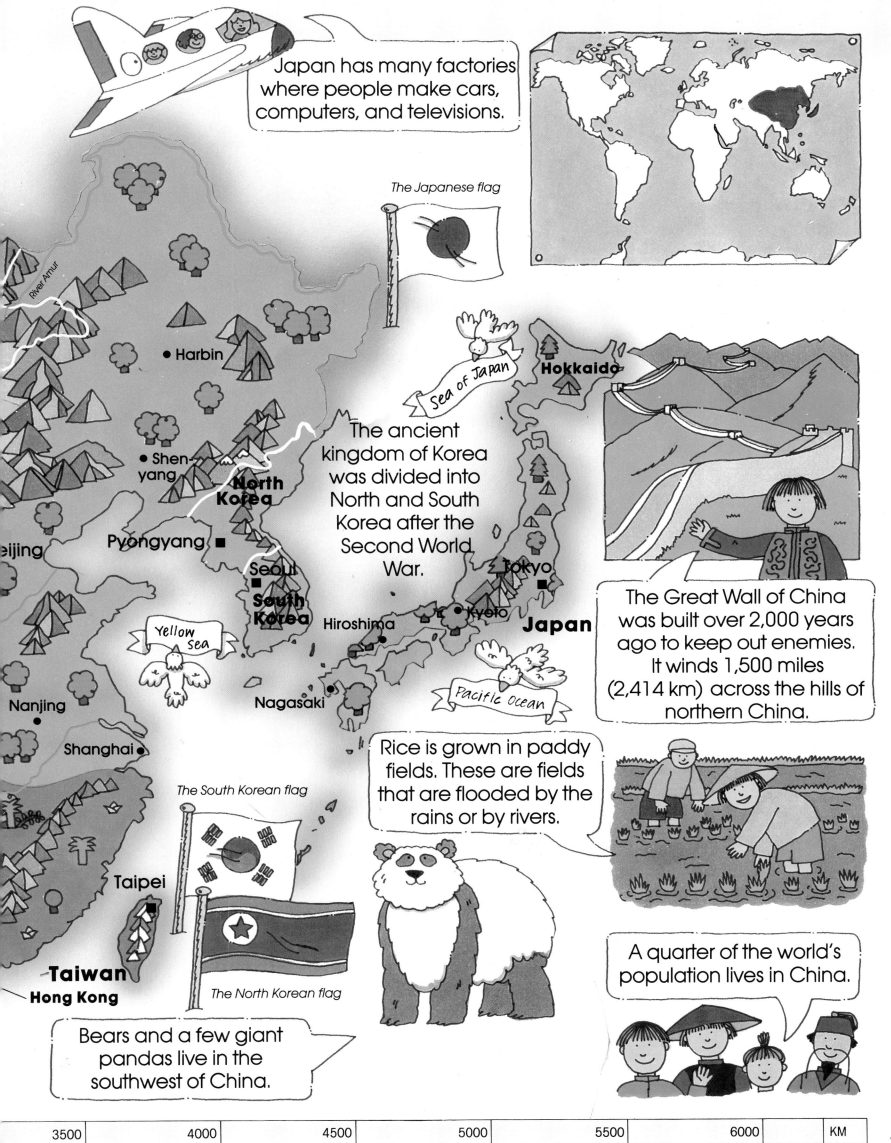

Japan has many factories where people make cars, computers, and televisions.

The Japanese flag

River Amur

Harbin

Shenyang

North Korea

eijing

Pyongyang

Sea of Japan

Hokkaido

The ancient kingdom of Korea was divided into North and South Korea after the Second World War.

Seoul

South Korea

Hiroshima

Tokyo

Kyoto

Japan

The Great Wall of China was built over 2,000 years ago to keep out enemies. It winds 1,500 miles (2,414 km) across the hills of northern China.

Yellow Sea

Nanjing

Shanghai

Nagasaki

Pacific Ocean

Rice is grown in paddy fields. These are fields that are flooded by the rains or by rivers.

The South Korean flag

Taipei

Taiwan

Hong Kong

The North Korean flag

A quarter of the world's population lives in China.

Bears and a few giant pandas live in the southwest of China.

| 3500 | 4000 | 4500 | 5000 | 5500 | 6000 | KM |
| | 2500 | | 3000 | | 3500 | MILES |

Australia and New Zealand

Australia is the smallest continent in the world. It lies in the southern Pacific Ocean, on the opposite side of the world from Europe. New Zealand is 900 miles (1,500km) southeast of Australia. Most of Australia is flat and dry. New Zealand is more hilly and green.

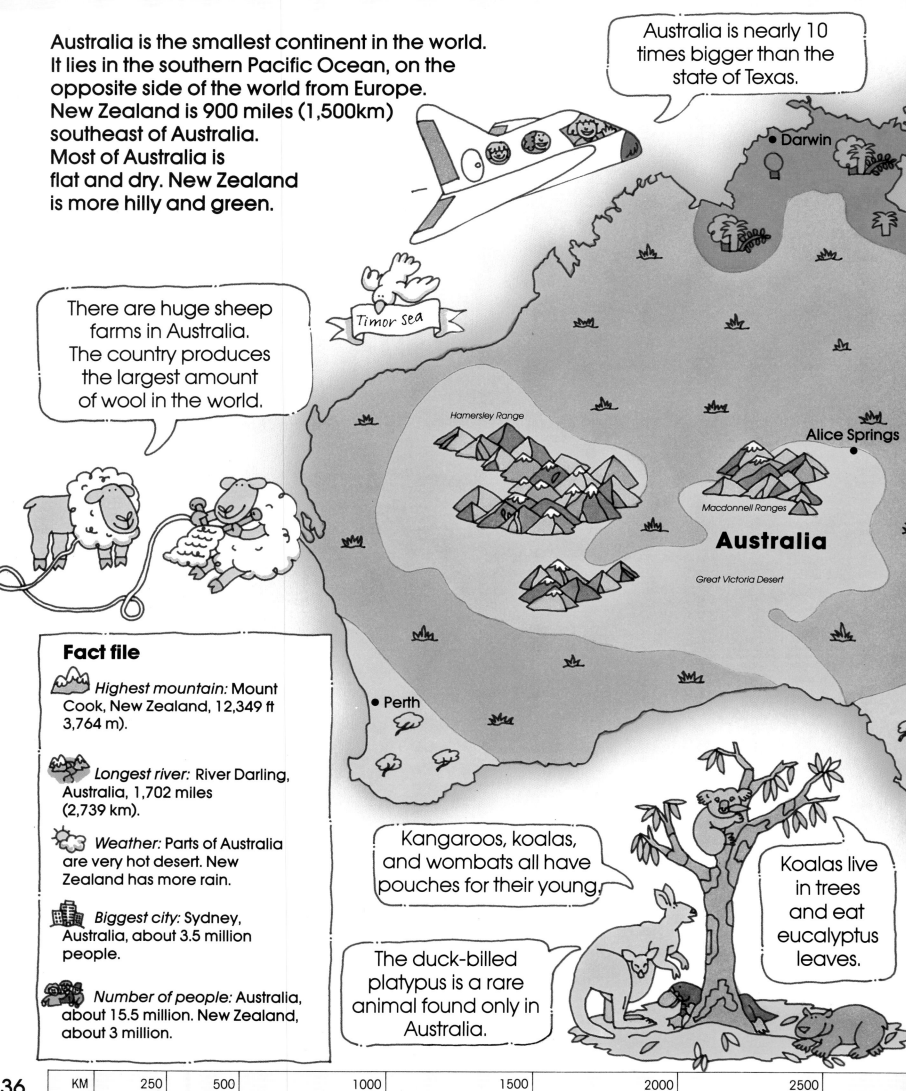

Australia is nearly 10 times bigger than the state of Texas.

There are huge sheep farms in Australia. The country produces the largest amount of wool in the world.

Timor Sea

Hamersley Range

Macdonnell Ranges

Alice Springs

Australia

Great Victoria Desert

Darwin

Perth

Fact file

Highest mountain: Mount Cook, New Zealand, 12,349 ft 3,764 m).

Longest river: River Darling, Australia, 1,702 miles (2,739 km).

Weather: Parts of Australia are very hot desert. New Zealand has more rain.

Biggest city: Sydney, Australia, about 3.5 million people.

Number of people: Australia, about 15.5 million. New Zealand, about 3 million.

Kangaroos, koalas, and wombats all have pouches for their young.

Koalas live in trees and eat eucalyptus leaves.

The duck-billed platypus is a rare animal found only in Australia.

KM	250	500	1000	1500	2000	2500
MILES	250	500	1000	1500		

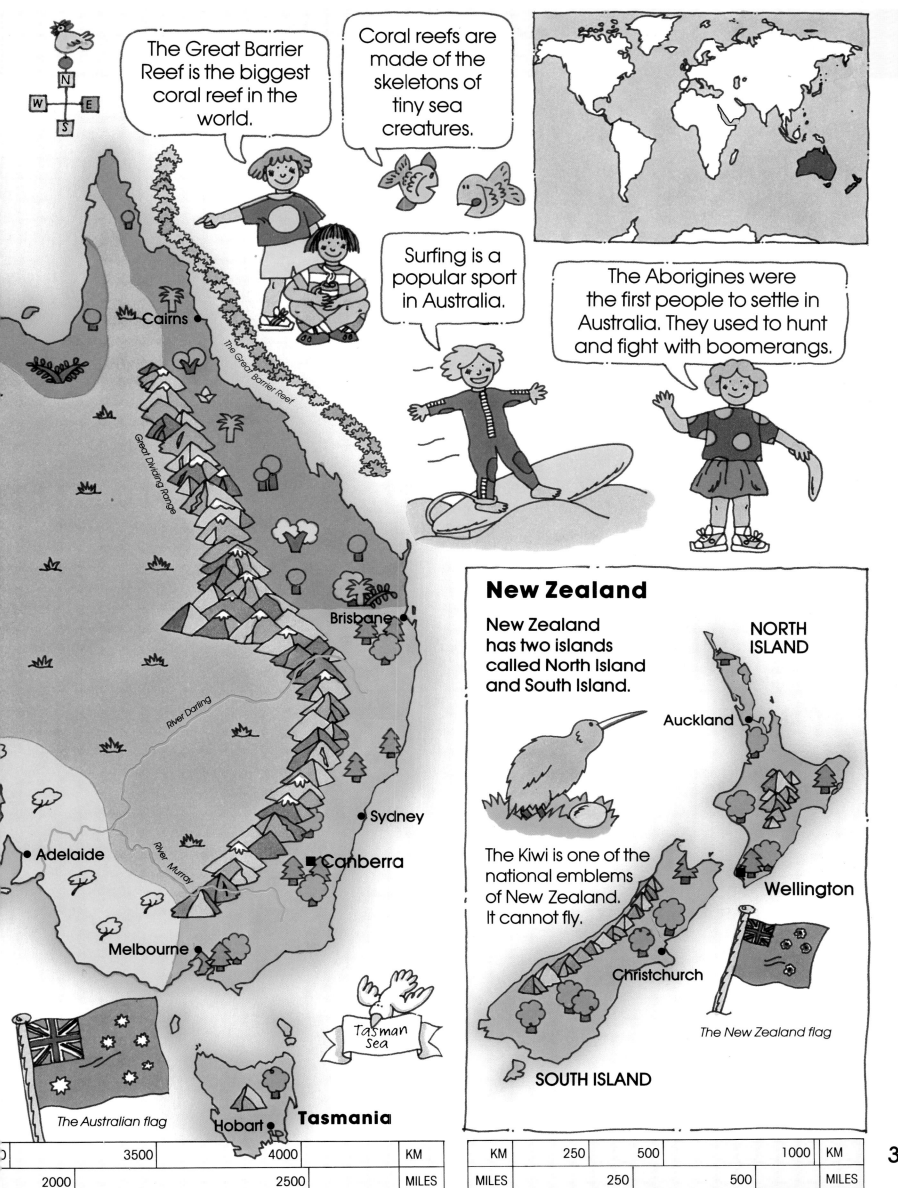

The Great Barrier Reef is the biggest coral reef in the world.

Coral reefs are made of the skeletons of tiny sea creatures.

Surfing is a popular sport in Australia.

The Aborigines were the first people to settle in Australia. They used to hunt and fight with boomerangs.

Cairns

The Great Barrier Reef

Great Dividing Range

Brisbane

River Darling

Sydney

Adelaide

River Murray

Canberra

Melbourne

Tasman Sea

The Australian flag

Hobart

Tasmania

New Zealand

New Zealand has two islands called North Island and South Island.

NORTH ISLAND

Auckland

The Kiwi is one of the national emblems of New Zealand. It cannot fly.

Wellington

Christchurch

The New Zealand flag

SOUTH ISLAND

	3500	4000	KM
2000		2500	MILES

KM	250	500	1000	KM
MILES		250	500	MILES

The Arctic

The Arctic is the area around the North Pole. It is frozen ocean surrounded by land. The ocean is covered with ice that slowly drifts from place to place.

The Icelandic flag

Polar bears live on the frozen sea. They catch seals to eat.

Alaska

Arctic Ocean

North Pole

Arctic Ocean

U.S.S.R.

Canada

Greenland

▪ Godthab

Sweden

Iceland
▪ Reykjavik

Arctic Circle

Finland

Norway

The Inuit live in the Arctic parts of Canada, Alaska, and Greenland.

In summer, most of the Arctic land is covered with plants. Grass and mosses grow there and many flowers bloom.

KM	250	500	1000	1500	2000	2500	3000	3500	4000	4500		KM
MILES		250	500	1000		1500		2000		2500		MILES

The Antarctic

The Antarctic is ice-covered land around the South Pole. The ice is 14,800 feet (4,500 meters) thick in some places. There are many high mountains and some volcanos.

At the North and South Poles, winter and summer last six months each. Winter is dark all day and night. In summer it is light all the time.

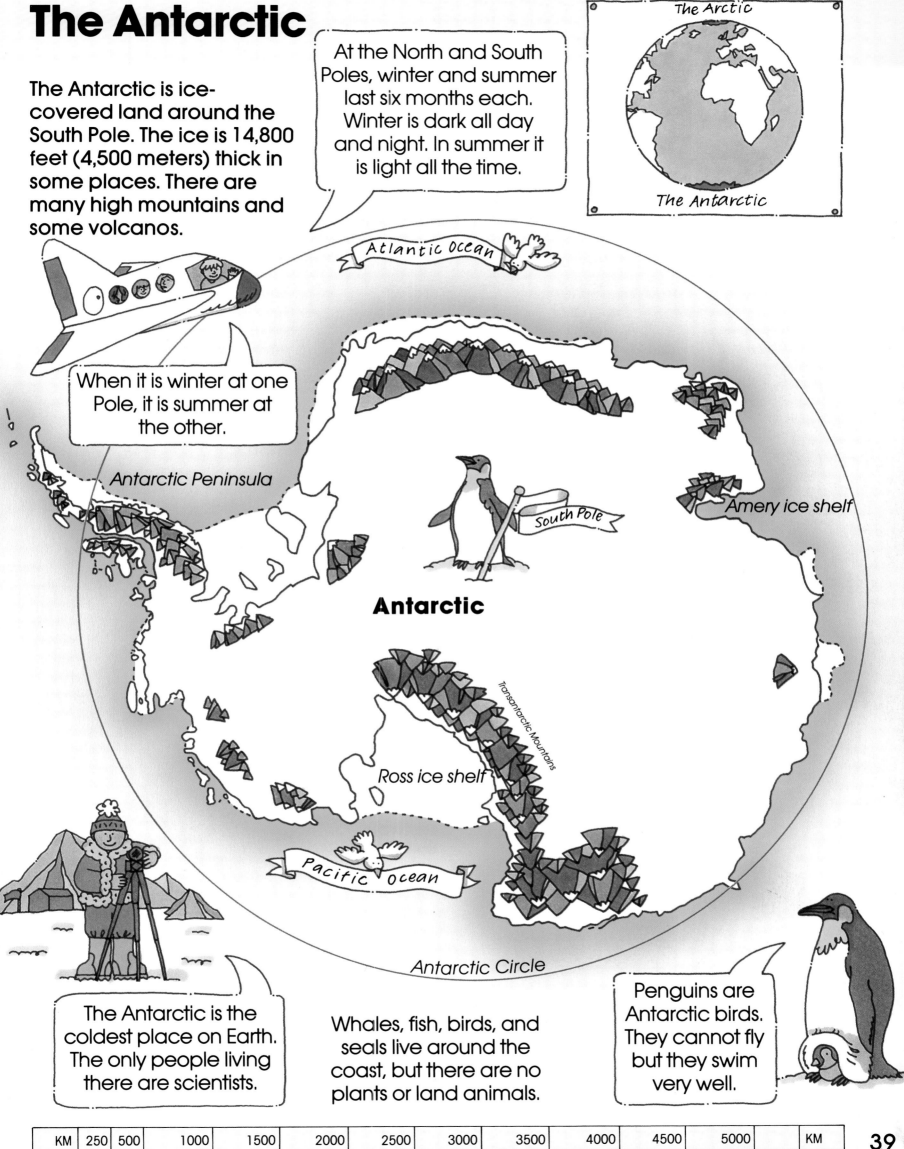

The Arctic

The Antarctic

When it is winter at one Pole, it is summer at the other.

Atlantic Ocean

Antarctic Peninsula

South Pole

Amery ice shelf

Antarctic

Transantarctic Mountains

Ross ice shelf

Pacific Ocean

Antarctic Circle

The Antarctic is the coldest place on Earth. The only people living there are scientists.

Whales, fish, birds, and seals live around the coast, but there are no plants or land animals.

Penguins are Antarctic birds. They cannot fly but they swim very well.

KM	250	500	1000	1500	2000	2500	3000	3500	4000	4500	5000	KM
MILES		250	500	1000		1500		2000		2500	3000		MILES

This book was created and produced by Times Four Publishing Ltd., High Street, Cuckfield, Sussex RH17 5EN.

Typeset by Amber Graphics, Burgess Hill, Sussex.
Colour separations by RCS Graphics Ltd., Leeds.
Printed by Proost, Belgium

Map consultants: Sussex University Map Library
Geography consultant: Diane Snowdon

Macmillan Publishing Company is part of the Maxwell Communication Group of Companies.

Macmillan Publishing Company
866 Third Avenue
New York, NY 10022

Maxwell Macmillan Canada, Inc.
1200 Eglinton Avenue East
Suite 200
Don Mills, Ontario M3C 3N1

First American edition

10 9 8 7 6 5 4 3 2 1

Library of Congress Cataloging-in-Publication Data is available.

ISBN 0-02-774920-7